INTRODUCTION TO
MATRIX
ALGEBRA

AUTAR KAW

http://www.autarkaw.com

*There is nothing noble about being superior
to another man; the true nobility lies in being
superior to your previous self* - Upanishads.

ISBN 978-0-615-25126-4

INTRODUCTION TO
MATRIX ALGEBRA

Second Edition

Autar Kaw
University of South Florida
http://www.autarkaw.com

To Sherrie, Candace and Angelie

THE AUTHOR

Autar K. Kaw is a Professor of Mechanical Engineering at the University of South Florida, Tampa. Professor Kaw obtained his B.E. (Hons.) degree in Mechanical Engineering from Birla Institute of Technology and Science, India in 1981. He received his Ph.D. degree in 1987 and M.S. degree in 1984, both in Engineering Mechanics from Clemson University, SC. He joined the faculty of University of South Florida, Tampa in 1987. He has also been a Maintenance Engineer (1982) for Ford-Escorts Tractors, India, and a Summer Faculty Fellow (1992) and Visiting Scientist (1991) at Wright Patterson Air Force Base.

Professor Kaw's main scholarly interests are in engineering education research, bridge design, thermal stresses, engineering software, computational nanomechanics, and fracture. His research has been funded by National Science Foundation, Air Force Office of Scientific Research, Florida Department of Transportation, Research and Development Laboratories, Systran Co, Wright Patterson Air Force Base, and Montgomery Tank Lines.

He is a Fellow of the American Society of Mechanical Engineers (ASME) and a member of the American Society of Engineering Education (ASEE). He has written more than forty journal papers and developed several software instructional programs for courses such as Mechanics of Composites and Numerical Methods.

Professor Kaw received the Florida Professor of the Year Award from the Council for Advancement and Support of Education (CASE) and Carnegie Foundation for Advancement of Teaching (CFAT) in 2004, American Society of Mechanical Engineers (ASME) Curriculum Innovation Award in 2004, Archie Higdon Mechanics Educator Award from the American Society of Engineering Education (ASEE) in 2003, State of Florida Teaching Incentive Program Award in 1994 and 1997, American Society of Engineering Education (ASEE) New Mechanics Educator Award in 1992, and the Society of Automotive Engineers (SAE) Ralph Teetor Award in 1991.

PREFACE

This book is an extended primer for undergraduate Matrix Algebra. The book is either to be used as a refresher material for students who have already taken a course in Matrix Algebra or as a just-in-time tool if the burden of teaching Matrix Algebra has been distributed to several courses. In my own department, the Linear Algebra course was dropped from the curriculum a decade ago. It is now taught just in time in courses like Statics, Programming Concepts, Vibrations, and Controls.

The book is divided into ten chapters. Chapter 1 defines the matrix and introduces you to special types of matrices. Chapter 2 deals with vectors and shows how to add and subtract vectors, find linear combination of vectors and how to find the rank of a set of vectors. Two types of operations are done on matrices. Chapter 3 explains binary operations of matrices such as adding, subtracting, multiplying and inverse of matrices. Chapter 4 describes the unary matrix operations such as transpose, trace, and determinant of matrices. Chapter 5 combines the concepts of the previous chapters to show how simultaneous linear equations are set up in a matrix form. The concept of the inverse of a matrix is introduced. The classification of a system of equations into a consistent (unique or multiple solutions) and inconsistent solutions (no solution) is established.

Chapters 6-8 deal with the numerical methods of solving simultaneous linear equations. Chapter 6 shows a direct method of solving equations such as the Gaussian elimination methods, Chapter 7 illustrates the iterative method of Gauss-Seidel method and Chapter 8 explains the LU Decomposition method.

Chapter 9 shows how a reader can determine that a solution to the simultaneous linear equations is adequate through the concept of condition number.

The last chapter - Chapter 10 discusses the concepts of eigenvalues and eigenvectors of a square matrix.

All chapters open with the objectives (what you will learn) followed by the content and numerous examples. At the end of each chapter, hyperlinked key terms, exercise set and answers to selected problems are given.

The book is available as a single pdf file or as a printed book in perfect binding. For details about price, please visit http://www.autarkaw.com/books/matrixalgebra/index.html. The book pdf file is interactive as it includes bookmarks and active hyperlinks within the document. The hyperlinks are available through the Table of Contents, Key Terms, references within the text, and the index. If you have any comments for the author, please send them to autarkaw@yahoo.com.

I am continuing to provide most of the resources free of charge while I am selling the book to gain sustainability as required by the sponsors via an extended electronic pdf file and the corresponding print version. The first eight chapters are part of the NSF funded

grants and are available free of charge as individual chapters at
http://numericalmethods.eng.usf.edu/matrixalgebrabook. The pdf file available for
download for a nominal fee has additional features of two extra chapters (Adequacy of
Solution and Eigenvalues/Eigenvectors), exercise sets, answers to selected problems,
table of contents, key terms, and index. Moreover, the pdf book is hyperlinked. You can
print the pdf file only for your personal use, while a perfect bound print-version of the
book is also available for a nominal charge.

I would like to thank Eric Marvella, Sri Harsha Garapati and Lauren Kintner for their
help in formatting the book. I would like to thank Matt Emmons and Luke Snyder for
developing and proofreading the solutions manual for the book, respectively. The
suggestions given by many users of the book have improved the quality and accuracy of
the book. I would like to thank my spouse, Sherrie and our children Candace and
Angelie, who have encouraged me throughout the project.

Book website: http://autarkaw.com/books/matrixalgebra/index.html

TABLE OF CONTENTS

CHAPTER 3   BINARY MATRIX OPERATIONS   32

CHAPTER 6   GAUSSIAN ELIMINATION   89

CHAPTER 10   EIGENVALUES AND EIGENVECTORS **154**

Chapter 04.01
Introduction

After reading this chapter, you should be able to

1. *define what a matrix is.*
2. *identify special types of matrices, and*
3. *identify when two matrices are equal.*

What does a matrix look like?

Matrices are everywhere. If you have used a spreadsheet such as Excel or Lotus or written a table, you have used a matrix. Matrices make presentation of numbers clearer and make calculations easier to program. Look at the matrix below about the sale of tires in a Blowoutr'us store – given by quarter and make of tires.

	Q1	Q2	Q3	Q4
Tirestone	25	20	3	2
Michigan	5	10	15	25
Copper	6	16	7	27

If one wants to know how many *Copper* tires were sold in *Quarter 4*, we go along the row *Copper* and column *Q4* and find that it is 27.

So what is a matrix?

A *matrix* is a rectangular array of elements. The elements can be symbolic expressions or numbers. Matrix $[A]$ is denoted by

$$[A] = \begin{bmatrix} a_{11} & a_{12} & \text{.......} & a_{1n} \\ a_{21} & a_{22} & \text{.......} & a_{2n} \\ \vdots & & & \vdots \\ a_{m1} & a_{m2} & \text{.......} & a_{mn} \end{bmatrix}$$

Row i of $[A]$ has n elements and is

$$[a_{i1} \quad a_{i2} .... a_{in}]$$

and column j of $[A]$ has m elements and is

$$\begin{bmatrix} a_{1j} \\ a_{2j} \\ \vdots \\ a_{mj} \end{bmatrix}$$

Each matrix has rows and columns and this defines the size of the matrix. If a matrix $[A]$ has m rows and n columns, the size of the matrix is denoted by $m \times n$. The matrix $[A]$ may also be denoted by $[A]_{m \times n}$ to show that $[A]$ is a matrix with m rows and n columns.

Each entry in the matrix is called the entry or element of the matrix and is denoted by a_{ij} where i is the row number and j is the column number of the element.

The matrix for the tire sales example could be denoted by the matrix $[A]$ as

$$[A] = \begin{bmatrix} 25 & 20 & 3 & 2 \\ 5 & 10 & 15 & 25 \\ 6 & 16 & 7 & 27 \end{bmatrix}.$$

There are 3 rows and 4 columns, so the size of the matrix is 3×4. In the above $[A]$ matrix, $a_{34} = 27$.

What are the special types of matrices?

Vector: A vector is a matrix that has only one row or one column. There are two types of vectors – row vectors and column vectors.

Row Vector:

If a matrix $[B]$ has one row, it is called a row vector $[B] = [b_1 \ b_2 ...... b_n]$ and n is the dimension of the row vector.

Example 1

Give an example of a row vector.
Solution

$$[B] = [25 \ 20 \ 3 \ 2 \ 0]$$

is an example of a row vector of dimension 5.

Column vector:

If a matrix $[C]$ has one column, it is called a column vector

$$[C] = \begin{bmatrix} c_1 \\ \vdots \\ \vdots \\ c_m \end{bmatrix}$$

and m is the dimension of the vector.

Example 2

Give an example of a column vector.
Solution

$$[C] = \begin{bmatrix} 25 \\ 5 \\ 6 \end{bmatrix}$$

is an example of a column vector of dimension 3.

Submatrix:

If some row(s) or/and column(s) of a matrix $[A]$ are deleted (no rows or columns may be deleted), the remaining matrix is called a submatrix of $[A]$.

Example 3

Find some of the submatrices of the matrix

$$[A] = \begin{bmatrix} 4 & 6 & 2 \\ 3 & -1 & 2 \end{bmatrix}$$

Solution

$$\begin{bmatrix} 4 & 6 & 2 \\ 3 & -1 & 2 \end{bmatrix}, \begin{bmatrix} 4 & 6 \\ 3 & -1 \end{bmatrix}, [4 \quad 6 \quad 2], [4], \begin{bmatrix} 2 \\ 2 \end{bmatrix}$$

are some of the submatrices of $[A]$. Can you find other submatrices of $[A]$?

Square matrix:

If the number of rows m of a matrix is equal to the number of columns n of a matrix $[A]$, ($m = n$), then $[A]$ is called a square matrix. The entries $a_{11}, a_{22}, ..., a_{nn}$ are called the *diagonal elements* of a square matrix. Sometimes the diagonal of the matrix is also called the *principal or main of the matrix*.

Example 4

Give an example of a square matrix.

Solution

$$[A] = \begin{bmatrix} 25 & 20 & 3 \\ 5 & 10 & 15 \\ 6 & 15 & 7 \end{bmatrix}$$

is a square matrix as it has the same number of rows and columns, that is, 3. The diagonal elements of $[A]$ are $a_{11} = 25$, $a_{22} = 10$, $a_{33} = 7$.

Upper triangular matrix:

A $m \times n$ matrix for which $a_{ij} = 0$, $i > j$ is called an upper triangular matrix. That is, all the elements below the diagonal entries are zero.

Example 5

Give an example of an upper triangular matrix.
Solution

$$[A] = \begin{bmatrix} 10 & -7 & 0 \\ 0 & -0.001 & 6 \\ 0 & 0 & 15005 \end{bmatrix}$$

is an upper triangular matrix.

Lower triangular matrix:

A $m \times n$ matrix for which $a_{ij} = 0$, $j > i$ is called a lower triangular matrix. That is, all the elements above the diagonal entries are zero.

Example 6

Give an example of a lower triangular matrix.
Solution

$$[A] = \begin{bmatrix} 1 & 0 & 0 \\ 0.3 & 1 & 0 \\ 0.6 & 2.5 & 1 \end{bmatrix}$$

is a lower triangular matrix.

Diagonal matrix:

A square matrix with all non-diagonal elements equal to zero is called a diagonal matrix, that is, only the diagonal entries of the square matrix can be non-zero, ($a_{ij} = 0$, $i \neq j$).

Example 7

Give examples of a diagonal matrix.

Solution

$$[A] = \begin{bmatrix} 3 & 0 & 0 \\ 0 & 2.1 & 0 \\ 0 & 0 & 0 \end{bmatrix}$$

is a diagonal matrix.

Any or all the diagonal entries of a diagonal matrix can be zero. For example

$$[A] = \begin{bmatrix} 3 & 0 & 0 \\ 0 & 2.1 & 0 \\ 0 & 0 & 0 \end{bmatrix}$$

is also a diagonal matrix.

Identity matrix:

A diagonal matrix with all diagonal elements equal to one is called an identity matrix, ($a_{ij} = 0$, $i \neq j$ and $a_{ii} = 1$ for all i).

Example 8

Give an example of an identity matrix.
Solution

$$[A] = \begin{bmatrix} 1 & 0 & 0 & 0 \\ 0 & 1 & 0 & 0 \\ 0 & 0 & 1 & 0 \\ 0 & 0 & 0 & 1 \end{bmatrix}$$

is an identity matrix.

Zero matrix:

A matrix whose all entries are zero is called a zero matrix, ($a_{ij} = 0$ for all i and j).

Example 9

Give examples of a zero matrix.
Solution

$$[A] = \begin{bmatrix} 0 & 0 & 0 \\ 0 & 0 & 0 \\ 0 & 0 & 0 \end{bmatrix}$$

$$[B] = \begin{bmatrix} 0 & 0 & 0 \\ 0 & 0 & 0 \end{bmatrix}$$

$$[C] = \begin{bmatrix} 0 & 0 & 0 & 0 \\ 0 & 0 & 0 & 0 \\ 0 & 0 & 0 & 0 \end{bmatrix}$$

$$[D] = \begin{bmatrix} 0 & 0 & 0 \end{bmatrix}$$

are all examples of a zero matrix.

Tridiagonal matrices:

A tridiagonal matrix is a square matrix in which all elements not on the following are zero - the major diagonal, the diagonal above the major diagonal, and the diagonal below the major diagonal.

Example 10

Give an example of a tridiagonal matrix.
Solution

$$[A] = \begin{bmatrix} 2 & 4 & 0 & 0 \\ 2 & 3 & 9 & 0 \\ 0 & 0 & 5 & 2 \\ 0 & 0 & 3 & 6 \end{bmatrix}$$

is a tridiagonal matrix.

Do non-square matrices have diagonal entries?

Yes, for a $m \times n$ matrix $[A]$, the diagonal entries are $a_{11}, a_{22} \ldots, a_{k-1,k-1}, a_{kk}$ where $k = \min\{m, n\}$.

Example 11

What are the diagonal entries of

$$[A] = \begin{bmatrix} 3.2 & 5 \\ 6 & 7 \\ 2.9 & 3.2 \\ 5.6 & 7.8 \end{bmatrix}$$

Solution

The diagonal elements of $[A]$ are $a_{11} = 3.2$ and $a_{22} = 7$.

Diagonally Dominant Matrix:

A $n \times n$ square matrix $[A]$ is a diagonally dominant matrix if

$$|a_{ii}| \geq \sum_{\substack{j=1 \\ i \neq j}}^{n} |a_{ij}| \text{ for all } i = 1, 2, \ldots, n \text{ and}$$

$$|a_{ii}| > \sum_{\substack{j=1 \\ i \neq j}}^{n} |a_{ij}| \quad \text{for at least one } i,$$

that is, for each row, the absolute value of the diagonal element is greater than or equal to the sum of the absolute values of the rest of the elements of that row, and that the inequality is strictly greater than for at least one row. Diagonally dominant matrices are important in ensuring convergence in iterative schemes of solving simultaneous linear equations.

Example 12

Give examples of diagonally dominant matrices and not diagonally dominant matrices.
Solution

$$[A] = \begin{bmatrix} 15 & 6 & 7 \\ 2 & -4 & -2 \\ 3 & 2 & 6 \end{bmatrix}$$

is a diagonally dominant matrix as

$$|a_{11}| = |15| = 15 \geq |a_{12}| + |a_{13}| = |6| + |7| = 13$$
$$|a_{22}| = |-4| = 4 \geq |a_{21}| + |a_{23}| = |2| + |-2| = 4$$
$$|a_{33}| = |6| = 6 \geq |a_{31}| + |a_{32}| = |3| + |2| = 5$$

and for at least one row, that is Rows 1 and 3 in this case, the inequality is a strictly greater than inequality.

$$[B] = \begin{bmatrix} -15 & 6 & 9 \\ 2 & -4 & 2 \\ 3 & -2 & 5.001 \end{bmatrix}$$

is a diagonally dominant matrix as

$$|b_{11}| = |-15| = 15 \geq |b_{12}| + |b_{13}| = |6| + |9| = 15$$
$$|b_{22}| = |-4| = 4 \geq |b_{21}| + |b_{23}| = |2| + |2| = 4$$
$$|b_{33}| = |5.001| = 5.001 \geq |b_{31}| + |b_{32}| = |3| + |-2| = 5$$

The inequalities are satisfied for all rows and it is satisfied strictly greater than for at least one row (in this case it is Row 3).

$$[C] = \begin{bmatrix} 25 & 5 & 1 \\ 64 & 8 & 1 \\ 144 & 12 & 1 \end{bmatrix}$$

is not diagonally dominant as

$$|c_{22}| = |8| = 8 \leq |c_{21}| + |c_{23}| = |64| + |1| = 65$$

When are two matrices considered to be equal?

Two matrices $[A]$ and $[B]$ are equal if the size of $[A]$ and $[B]$ is the same (number of rows and columns are same for $[A]$ and $[B]$) and $a_{ij} = b_{ij}$ for all i and j.

Example 13

What would make

$$[A] = \begin{bmatrix} 2 & 3 \\ 6 & 7 \end{bmatrix}$$

to be equal to

$$[B] = \begin{bmatrix} b_{11} & 3 \\ 6 & b_{22} \end{bmatrix}$$

Solution

The two matrices $[A]$ and $[B]$ ould be equal if $b_{11} = 2$ and $b_{22} = 7$.

Key Terms:

Matrix
Vector
Submatrix
Square matrix
Equal matrices
Zero matrix
Identity matrix
Diagonal matrix
Upper triangular matrix
Lower triangular matrix
Tri-diagonal matrix
Diagonally dominant matrix

Problem Set

Chapter 04.01
Introduction

1. Write an example of a row vector of dimension 4.

2. Write an example of a column vector of dimension 4.

3. Write an example of a square matrix of order 4×4.

4. Write an example of a tri-diagonal matrix of order 4×4.

5. Write an example of a identity matrix of order 5×5.

6. Write an example of a upper triangular matrix of order 4×4.

7. Write an example of a lower triangular matrix of order 4×4.

8. Which of these matrices are strictly diagonally dominant?

$$(A) \quad [A] = \begin{bmatrix} 15 & 6 & 7 \\ 2 & -4 & 2 \\ 3 & 2 & 6 \end{bmatrix}$$

$$(B) \quad [A] = \begin{bmatrix} 5 & 6 & 7 \\ 2 & -4 & 2 \\ 3 & 2 & -5 \end{bmatrix}$$

$$(C) \quad [A] = \begin{bmatrix} 5 & 3 & 2 \\ 6 & -8 & 2 \\ 7 & -5 & 12 \end{bmatrix}$$

9. Find all the submatrices of
$$[A] = \begin{bmatrix} 10 & -7 & 0 \\ 0 & -0.001 & 6 \end{bmatrix}$$

10. If
$$[A] = \begin{bmatrix} 4 & -1 \\ 0 & 2 \end{bmatrix},$$
what are b_{11} and b_{12} in

$$[B] = \begin{bmatrix} b_{11} & b_{12} \\ 0 & 4 \end{bmatrix}$$

if $[B] = 2[A]$.

11. Are matrix

$$[A] = \begin{bmatrix} 10 & -7 & 0 \\ 0 & -0.001 & 6 \end{bmatrix}$$

and matrix

$$[B] = \begin{bmatrix} 10 & 0 \\ -7 & -0.001 \\ 0 & 6 \end{bmatrix}$$

equal?

12. A square matrix $[A]$ is lower triangular if

    (A) $a_{ij} = 0$ for $i > j$

    (B) $a_{ij} = 0$ for $j > i$

    (C) $a_{ij} = 0$ for $i = j$

    (D) $a_{ij} = 0$ for $i + j = \text{odd integer}$

13. A square matrix $[A]$ is upper triangular if

    (A) $a_{ij} = 0$ for $i > j$

    (B) $a_{ij} = 0$ for $j > i$

    (C) $a_{ij} = 0$ for $i = j$

$a_{ij} = 0$ for $i + j = \text{odd integer}$

Answers to Selected Problems:

1. $\begin{bmatrix} 5 & 6 & 2 & 3 \end{bmatrix}$

2. $\begin{bmatrix} 5 \\ -7 \\ 3 \\ 2.5 \end{bmatrix}$

3. $\begin{bmatrix} 9 & 0 & -2 & 3 \\ -2 & 3 & 5 & 1 \\ 1.5 & 6 & 7 & 8 \\ 1.1 & 2 & 3 & 4 \end{bmatrix}$

4. $\begin{bmatrix} 6 & 3 & 0 & 0 \\ 2.1 & 2 & 2.2 & 0 \\ 0 & 6.2 & -3 & 3.5 \\ 0 & 0 & 2.1 & 4.1 \end{bmatrix}$

5. $\begin{bmatrix} 1 & 0 & 0 & 0 & 0 \\ 0 & 1 & 0 & 0 & 0 \\ 0 & 0 & 1 & 0 & 0 \\ 0 & 0 & 0 & 1 & 0 \\ 0 & 0 & 0 & 0 & 1 \end{bmatrix}$

6. $\begin{bmatrix} 6 & 2 & 3 & 9 \\ 0 & 1 & 2 & 3 \\ 0 & 0 & 4 & 5 \\ 0 & 0 & 0 & 6 \end{bmatrix}$

7. $\begin{bmatrix} 2 & 0 & 0 & 0 \\ 3 & 1 & 0 & 0 \\ 4 & 2 & 4 & 0 \\ 5 & 3 & 5 & 6 \end{bmatrix}$

8. (A) Yes   (B) No   (C) No

9. $\begin{bmatrix} 10 \end{bmatrix}$ $\begin{bmatrix} -7 \end{bmatrix}$ $\begin{bmatrix} 0 \end{bmatrix}$, $\begin{bmatrix} 0 \end{bmatrix}$, $\begin{bmatrix} -0.001 \end{bmatrix}$, $\begin{bmatrix} 6 \end{bmatrix}$

$$\begin{bmatrix} 10 \\ 0 \end{bmatrix}, \begin{bmatrix} -7 \\ -.001 \end{bmatrix}, \begin{bmatrix} 0 \\ 6 \end{bmatrix}, \begin{bmatrix} 10 & -7 & 0 \end{bmatrix}, \begin{bmatrix} 0 & -0.001 & 6 \end{bmatrix}, \begin{bmatrix} 10 & -7 \\ 0 & -0.001 \end{bmatrix}, \begin{bmatrix} 10 & 0 \\ 0 & 6 \end{bmatrix},$$

$$\begin{bmatrix} -7 & 0 \\ -0.001 & 6 \end{bmatrix}, \begin{bmatrix} 10,-7 \end{bmatrix}, \begin{bmatrix} 10,0 \end{bmatrix}, \begin{bmatrix} -7,0 \end{bmatrix}, \begin{bmatrix} 0,6 \end{bmatrix}, \begin{bmatrix} 0,-0.001 \end{bmatrix}, \begin{bmatrix} -0.001,6 \end{bmatrix}.$$

10. 8,–2

11. No

12. B

13. A

Chapter 04.02
Vectors

After reading this chapter, you should be able to:

1. *define a vector,*
2. *add and subtract vectors,*
3. *find linear combinations of vectors and their relationship to a set of equations,*
4. *explain what it means to have a linearly independent set of vectors, and*
5. *find the rank of a set of vectors.*

What is a vector?

A vector is a collection of numbers in a definite order. If it is a collection of n numbers, it is called a n-dimensional vector. So the vector $\vec{A}$ given by

$$\vec{A} = \begin{bmatrix} a_1 \\ a_2 \\ \vdots \\ a_n \end{bmatrix}$$

is a n-dimensional column vector with n components, $a_1, a_2, \ldots, a_n$. The above is a column vector. A row vector $[B]$ is of the form $\vec{B} = [b_1, b_2, \ldots, b_n]$ where $\vec{B}$ is a n-dimensional row vector with n components $b_1, b_2, \ldots, b_n$.

Example 1

Give an example of a 3-dimensional column vector.
Solution

Assume a point in space is given by its (x, y, z) coordinates. Then if the value of $x = 3, y = 2, z = 5$, the column vector corresponding to the location of the points is

$$\begin{bmatrix} x \\ y \\ z \end{bmatrix} = \begin{bmatrix} 3 \\ 2 \\ 5 \end{bmatrix}.$$

04.02.1

When are two vectors equal?

Two vectors $\vec{A}$ and $\vec{B}$ are equal if they are of the same dimension and if their corresponding components are equal.
Given

$$\vec{A} = \begin{bmatrix} a_1 \\ a_2 \\ \vdots \\ a_n \end{bmatrix}$$

and

$$\vec{B} = \begin{bmatrix} b_1 \\ b_2 \\ \vdots \\ b_n \end{bmatrix}$$

then $\vec{A} = \vec{B}$ if $a_i = b_i$, $i = 1,2,\ldots\ldots,n$.

Example 2

What are the values of the unknown components in $\vec{B}$ if

$$\vec{A} = \begin{bmatrix} 2 \\ 3 \\ 4 \\ 1 \end{bmatrix}$$

and

$$\vec{B} = \begin{bmatrix} b_1 \\ 3 \\ 4 \\ b_4 \end{bmatrix}$$

and $\vec{A} = \vec{B}$.
Solution

$$b_1 = 2, b_4 = 1$$

How do you add two vectors?

Two vectors can be added only if they are of the same dimension and the addition is given by

$$[A]+[B] = \begin{bmatrix} a_1 \\ a_2 \\ \vdots \\ a_n \end{bmatrix} + \begin{bmatrix} b_1 \\ b_2 \\ \vdots \\ b_n \end{bmatrix}$$

$$= \begin{bmatrix} a_1 + b_1 \\ a_2 + b_2 \\ \vdots \\ a_n + b_n \end{bmatrix}$$

Example 3

Add the two vectors

$$\vec{A} = \begin{bmatrix} 2 \\ 3 \\ 4 \\ 1 \end{bmatrix}$$

and

$$\vec{B} = \begin{bmatrix} 5 \\ -2 \\ 3 \\ 7 \end{bmatrix}$$

Solution

$$\vec{A} + \vec{B} = \begin{bmatrix} 2 \\ 3 \\ 4 \\ 1 \end{bmatrix} + \begin{bmatrix} 5 \\ -2 \\ 3 \\ 7 \end{bmatrix}$$

$$= \begin{bmatrix} 2+5 \\ 3-2 \\ 4+3 \\ 1+7 \end{bmatrix}$$

$$= \begin{bmatrix} 7 \\ 1 \\ 7 \\ 8 \end{bmatrix}$$

Example 4

A store sells three brands of tires: Tirestone, Michigan and Copper. In quarter 1, the sales are given by the column vector

$$\vec{A}_1 = \begin{bmatrix} 25 \\ 5 \\ 6 \end{bmatrix}$$

where the rows represent the three brands of tires sold – Tirestone, Michigan and Copper respectively. In quarter 2, the sales are given by

$$\vec{A}_2 = \begin{bmatrix} 20 \\ 10 \\ 6 \end{bmatrix}$$

What is the total sale of each brand of tire in the first half of the year?
Solution

The total sales would be given by

$$\vec{C} = \vec{A}_1 + \vec{A}_2$$

$$= \begin{bmatrix} 25 \\ 5 \\ 6 \end{bmatrix} + \begin{bmatrix} 20 \\ 10 \\ 6 \end{bmatrix}$$

$$= \begin{bmatrix} 25 + 20 \\ 5 + 10 \\ 6 + 6 \end{bmatrix}$$

$$= \begin{bmatrix} 45 \\ 15 \\ 12 \end{bmatrix}$$

So the number of Tirestone tires sold is 45, Michigan is 15 and Copper is 12 in the first half of the year.

What is a null vector?

A null vector is where all the components of the vector are zero.

Example 5

Give an example of a null vector or zero vector.
Solution

The vector

$$\begin{bmatrix} 0 \\ 0 \\ 0 \\ 0 \end{bmatrix}$$

is an example of a zero or null vector.

What is a unit vector?

A unit vector $\vec{U}$ is defined as

$$\vec{U} = \begin{bmatrix} u_1 \\ u_2 \\ \vdots \\ u_n \end{bmatrix}$$

where

$$\sqrt{u_1^2 + u_2^2 + u_3^2 + \ldots + u_n^2} = 1$$

Example 6

Give examples of 3-dimensional unit column vectors.
Solution

Examples include

$$\begin{bmatrix} \dfrac{1}{\sqrt{3}} \\ \dfrac{1}{\sqrt{3}} \\ \dfrac{1}{\sqrt{3}} \end{bmatrix}, \begin{bmatrix} 1 \\ 0 \\ 0 \end{bmatrix}, \begin{bmatrix} \dfrac{1}{\sqrt{2}} \\ \dfrac{1}{\sqrt{2}} \\ 0 \end{bmatrix}, \begin{bmatrix} 0 \\ 1 \\ 0 \end{bmatrix}, \text{etc.}$$

How do you multiply a vector by a scalar?

If k is a scalar and $\vec{A}$ is a n-dimensional vector, then

$$k\vec{A} = k\begin{bmatrix} a_1 \\ a_2 \\ \vdots \\ a_n \end{bmatrix}$$

$$= \begin{bmatrix} ka_1 \\ ka_2 \\ \vdots \\ ka_n \end{bmatrix}$$

Example 7

What is $2\vec{A}$ if

$$\vec{A} = \begin{bmatrix} 25 \\ 20 \\ 5 \end{bmatrix}$$

Solution

$$2\vec{A} = 2\begin{bmatrix} 25 \\ 20 \\ 5 \end{bmatrix}$$

$$= \begin{bmatrix} 2 \times 25 \\ 2 \times 20 \\ 2 \times 5 \end{bmatrix}$$

$$= \begin{bmatrix} 50 \\ 40 \\ 10 \end{bmatrix}$$

Example 8

A store sells three brands of tires: Tirestone, Michigan and Copper. In quarter 1, the sales are given by the column vector

$$\vec{A} = \begin{bmatrix} 25 \\ 25 \\ 6 \end{bmatrix}$$

If the goal is to increase the sales of all tires by at least 25% in the next quarter, how many of each brand should be sold?

Solution

Since the goal is to increase the sales by 25%, one would multiply the $\vec{A}$ vector by 1.25,

$$\vec{B} = 1.25\begin{bmatrix} 25 \\ 25 \\ 6 \end{bmatrix}$$

$$= \begin{bmatrix} 31.25 \\ 31.25 \\ 7.5 \end{bmatrix}$$

Since the number of tires must be an integer, we can say that the goal of sales is

$$\vec{B} = \begin{bmatrix} 32 \\ 32 \\ 8 \end{bmatrix}$$

What do you mean by a linear combination of vectors?

Given

$$\vec{A}_1, \vec{A}_2, \ldots, \vec{A}_m$$

as m vectors of same dimension n, and if k_1, k_2, ..., k_m are scalars, then

$$k_1 \vec{A}_1 + k_2 \vec{A}_2 + \ldots + k_m \vec{A}_m$$

is a linear combination of the m vectors.

Example 9

Find the linear combinations

a) $\vec{A} - \vec{B}$ and

b) $\vec{A} + \vec{B} - 3\vec{C}$

where

$$\vec{A} = \begin{bmatrix} 2 \\ 3 \\ 6 \end{bmatrix}, \vec{B} = \begin{bmatrix} 1 \\ 1 \\ 2 \end{bmatrix}, \vec{C} = \begin{bmatrix} 10 \\ 1 \\ 2 \end{bmatrix}$$

Solution

a) $\vec{A} - \vec{B} = \begin{bmatrix} 2 \\ 3 \\ 6 \end{bmatrix} - \begin{bmatrix} 1 \\ 1 \\ 2 \end{bmatrix}$

$= \begin{bmatrix} 2-1 \\ 3-1 \\ 6-2 \end{bmatrix}$

$= \begin{bmatrix} 1 \\ 2 \\ 4 \end{bmatrix}$

b) $\vec{A} + \vec{B} - 3\vec{C} = \begin{bmatrix} 2 \\ 3 \\ 6 \end{bmatrix} + \begin{bmatrix} 1 \\ 1 \\ 2 \end{bmatrix} - 3\begin{bmatrix} 10 \\ 1 \\ 2 \end{bmatrix}$

$= \begin{bmatrix} 2+1-30 \\ 3+1-3 \\ 6+2-6 \end{bmatrix}$

$= \begin{bmatrix} -27 \\ 1 \\ 2 \end{bmatrix}$

What do you mean by vectors being linearly independent?

A set of vectors $\vec{A}_1, \vec{A}_2, \ldots, \vec{A}_m$ are considered to be linearly independent if

$$k_1\vec{A}_1 + k_2\vec{A}_2 + \ldots\ldots + k_m\vec{A}_m = \vec{0}$$

has only one solution of

$$k_1 = k_2 = \ldots\ldots = k_m = 0$$

Example 10

Are the three vectors

$$\vec{A}_1 = \begin{bmatrix} 25 \\ 64 \\ 144 \end{bmatrix}, \vec{A}_2 = \begin{bmatrix} 5 \\ 8 \\ 12 \end{bmatrix}, \vec{A}_3 = \begin{bmatrix} 1 \\ 1 \\ 1 \end{bmatrix}$$

linearly independent?

Solution

Writing the linear combination of the three vectors

$$k_1\begin{bmatrix} 25 \\ 64 \\ 144 \end{bmatrix} + k_2\begin{bmatrix} 5 \\ 8 \\ 12 \end{bmatrix} + k_3\begin{bmatrix} 1 \\ 1 \\ 1 \end{bmatrix} = \begin{bmatrix} 0 \\ 0 \\ 0 \end{bmatrix}$$

gives

$$\begin{bmatrix} 25k_1 + 5k_2 + k_3 \\ 64k_1 + 8k_2 + k_3 \\ 144k_1 + 12k_2 + k_3 \end{bmatrix} = \begin{bmatrix} 0 \\ 0 \\ 0 \end{bmatrix}$$

The above equations have only one solution, $k_1 = k_2 = k_3 = 0$. However, how do we show that this is the only solution? This is shown below.
The above equations are

$$25k_1 + 5k_2 + k_3 = 0 \tag{1}$$

$$64k_1 + 8k_2 + k_3 = 0 \tag{2}$$

$$144k_1 + 12k_2 + k_3 = 0 \tag{3}$$

Subtracting Eqn (1) from Eqn (2) gives

$$39k_1 + 3k_2 = 0$$

$$k_2 = -13k_1 \tag{4}$$

Multiplying Eqn (1) by 8 and subtracting it from Eqn (2) that is first multiplied by 5 gives

$$120k_1 - 3k_3 = 0$$

$$k_3 = 40k_1 \tag{5}$$

Remember we found Eqn (4) and Eqn (5) just from Eqns (1) and (2).
Substitution of Eqns (4) and (5) in Eqn (3) for k_1 and k_2 gives

$$144k_1 + 12(-13k_1) + 40k_1 = 0$$

$$28k_1 = 0$$

$$k_1 = 0$$

This means that k_1 has to be zero, and coupled with (4) and (5), k_2 and k_3 are also zero. So the only solution is $k_1 = k_2 = k_3 = 0$. The three vectors hence are linearly independent.

Example 11

Are the three vectors

$$\vec{A}_1 = \begin{bmatrix} 1 \\ 2 \\ 5 \end{bmatrix}, \vec{A}_2 = \begin{bmatrix} 2 \\ 5 \\ 7 \end{bmatrix}, A_3 = \begin{bmatrix} 6 \\ 14 \\ 24 \end{bmatrix}$$

linearly independent?
Solution

By inspection,

$$\vec{A}_3 = 2\vec{A}_1 + 2\vec{A}_2$$

or

$$-2\vec{A}_1 - 2\vec{A}_2 + \vec{A}_3 = \vec{0}$$

So the linear combination

$$k_1\vec{A}_1 + k_2\vec{A}_2 + k_3\vec{A}_3 = \vec{0}$$

has a non-zero solution

$$k_1 = -2, k_2 = -2, k_3 = 1$$

Hence, the set of vectors is linearly dependent.
What if I cannot prove by inspection, what do I do? Put the linear combination of three vectors equal to the zero vector,

$$k_1 \begin{bmatrix} 1 \\ 2 \\ 5 \end{bmatrix} + k_2 \begin{bmatrix} 2 \\ 5 \\ 7 \end{bmatrix} + k_3 \begin{bmatrix} 6 \\ 14 \\ 24 \end{bmatrix} = \begin{bmatrix} 0 \\ 0 \\ 0 \end{bmatrix}$$

to give

$$k_1 + 2k_2 + 6k_3 = 0 \tag{1}$$
$$2k_1 + 5k_2 + 14k_3 = 0 \tag{2}$$
$$5k_1 + 7k_2 + 24k_3 = 0 \tag{3}$$

Multiplying Eqn (1) by 2 and subtracting from Eqn (2) gives

$$k_2 + 2k_3 = 0$$
$$k_2 = -2k_3 \tag{4}$$

Multiplying Eqn (1) by 2.5 and subtracting from Eqn (2) gives

$$-0.5k_1 - k_3 = 0$$
$$k_1 = -2k_3 \tag{5}$$

Remember we found Eqn (4) and Eqn (5) just from Eqns (1) and (2).
Substitute Eqn (4) and (5) in Eqn (3) for k_1 and k_2 gives

$$5(-2k_3) + 7(-2k_3) + 24k_3 = 0$$

$$-10k_3 - 14k_3 + 24k_3 = 0$$
$$0 = 0$$

This means any values satisfying Eqns (4) and (5) will satisfy Eqns (1), (2) and (3) simultaneously.

For example, chose

$k_3 = 6$, then

$k_2 = -12$ from Eqn (4), and

$k_1 = -12$ from Eqn (5).

Hence we have a nontrivial solution of $\begin{bmatrix} k_1 & k_2 & k_3 \end{bmatrix} = \begin{bmatrix} -12 & -12 & 6 \end{bmatrix}$. This implies the three given vectors are linearly dependent. Can you find another nontrivial solution?

What about the following three vectors?

$$\begin{bmatrix} 1 \\ 2 \\ 5 \end{bmatrix}, \begin{bmatrix} 2 \\ 5 \\ 7 \end{bmatrix}, \begin{bmatrix} 6 \\ 14 \\ 25 \end{bmatrix}$$

Are they linearly dependent or linearly independent?

Note that the only difference between this set of vectors and the previous one is the third entry in the third vector. Hence, equations (4) and (5) are still valid. What conclusion do you draw when you plug in equations (4) and (5) in the third equation: $5k_1 + 7k_2 + 25k_3 = 0$? What has changed?

Example 12

Are the three vectors

$$\vec{A}_1 = \begin{bmatrix} 25 \\ 64 \\ 89 \end{bmatrix}, \vec{A}_2 = \begin{bmatrix} 5 \\ 8 \\ 13 \end{bmatrix}, \vec{A}_3 = \begin{bmatrix} 1 \\ 1 \\ 2 \end{bmatrix}$$

linearly independent?

Solution

Writing the linear combination of the three vectors and equating to zero vector

$$k_1 \begin{bmatrix} 25 \\ 64 \\ 89 \end{bmatrix} + k_2 \begin{bmatrix} 5 \\ 8 \\ 13 \end{bmatrix} + k_3 \begin{bmatrix} 1 \\ 1 \\ 2 \end{bmatrix} = \begin{bmatrix} 0 \\ 0 \\ 0 \end{bmatrix}$$

gives

$$\begin{bmatrix} 25k_1 + 5k_2 + k_3 \\ 64k_1 + 8k_2 + k_3 \\ 89k_1 + 13k_2 + 2k_3 \end{bmatrix} = \begin{bmatrix} 0 \\ 0 \\ 0 \end{bmatrix}$$

In addition to $k_1 = k_2 = k_3 = 0$, one can find other solutions for which k_1, k_2, k_3 are not equal to zero. For example $k_1 = 1, k_2 = -13, k_3 = 40$ is also a solution. This implies

$$1\begin{bmatrix} 25 \\ 64 \\ 89 \end{bmatrix} - 13\begin{bmatrix} 5 \\ 8 \\ 13 \end{bmatrix} + 40\begin{bmatrix} 1 \\ 1 \\ 2 \end{bmatrix} = \begin{bmatrix} 0 \\ 0 \\ 0 \end{bmatrix}$$

So the linear combination that gives us a zero vector consists of non-zero constants. Hence $\vec{A_1}, \vec{A_2}, \vec{A_3}$ are linearly dependent.

What do you mean by the rank of a set of vectors?

From a set of n-dimensional vectors, the maximum number of linearly independent vectors in the set is called the rank of the set of vectors. *Note that the rank of the vectors can never be greater than the vectors dimension.*

Example 13

What is the rank of

$$\vec{A_1} = \begin{bmatrix} 25 \\ 64 \\ 144 \end{bmatrix}, \vec{A_2} = \begin{bmatrix} 5 \\ 8 \\ 12 \end{bmatrix}, \vec{A_3} = \begin{bmatrix} 1 \\ 1 \\ 1 \end{bmatrix}?$$

Solution

Since we found in Example 2.10 that $\vec{A_1}, \vec{A_2}, \vec{A_3}$ are linearly independent, the rank of the set of vectors $\vec{A_1}, \vec{A_2}, \vec{A_3}$ is 3.

Example 14

What is the rank of

$$\vec{A_1} = \begin{bmatrix} 25 \\ 64 \\ 89 \end{bmatrix}, \vec{A_2} = \begin{bmatrix} 5 \\ 8 \\ 13 \end{bmatrix}, \vec{A_3} = \begin{bmatrix} 1 \\ 1 \\ 2 \end{bmatrix}?$$

Solution

In Example 2.12, we found that $\vec{A_1}, \vec{A_2}, \vec{A_3}$ are linearly dependent, the rank of $\vec{A_1}, \vec{A_2}, \vec{A_3}$ is hence not 3, and is less than 3. Is it 2? Let us choose

$$\vec{A_1} = \begin{bmatrix} 25 \\ 64 \\ 89 \end{bmatrix}, \vec{A_2} = \begin{bmatrix} 5 \\ 8 \\ 13 \end{bmatrix}$$

Linear combination of $\vec{A_1}$ and $\vec{A_2}$ equal to zero has only one solution. Therefore, the rank is 2.

Example 15

What is the rank of

$$\vec{A}_1 = \begin{bmatrix} 1 \\ 1 \\ 2 \end{bmatrix}, \vec{A}_2 = \begin{bmatrix} 2 \\ 2 \\ 4 \end{bmatrix}, \vec{A}_3 = \begin{bmatrix} 3 \\ 3 \\ 5 \end{bmatrix}?$$

Solution

From inspection,

$$\vec{A}_2 = 2\vec{A}_1,$$

that implies

$$2\vec{A}_1 - \vec{A}_2 + 0\vec{A}_3 = \vec{0}.$$

Hence

$$k_1\vec{A}_1 + k_2\vec{A}_2 + k_3\vec{A}_3 = \vec{0}.$$

has a nontrivial solution.

So $\vec{A}_1, \vec{A}_2, \vec{A}_3$ are linearly dependent, and hence the rank of the three vectors is not 3. Since

$$\vec{A}_2 = 2\vec{A}_1,$$

$\vec{A}_1$ and $\vec{A}_2$ are linearly dependent, but

$$k_1\vec{A}_1 + k_3\vec{A}_3 = \vec{0}.$$

has trivial solution as the only solution. So $\vec{A}_1$ and $\vec{A}_3$ are linearly independent. The rank of the above three vectors is 2.

Prove that if a set of vectors contains the null vector, the set of vectors is linearly dependent.

Let $\vec{A}_1, \vec{A}_2, \dots\dots, \vec{A}_m$ be a set of n-dimensional vectors, then

$$k_1\vec{A}_1 + k_2\vec{A}_2 + \dots + k_m\vec{A}_m = \vec{0}$$

is a linear combination of the m vectors. Then assuming if $\vec{A}_1$ is the zero or null vector, any value of k_1 coupled with $k_2 = k_3 = \dots = k_m = 0$ will satisfy the above equation. Hence, the set of vectors is linearly dependent as more than one solution exists.

Prove that if a set of vectors are linearly independent, then a subset of the m vectors also has to be linearly independent.

Let this subset be

$$\vec{A}_{a1}, \vec{A}_{a2}, \dots, \vec{A}_{ap}$$

where $p < m$.

Then if this subset is linearly dependent, the linear combination

$$k_1\vec{A}_{a1} + k_2\vec{A}_{a2} + \dots + k_p\vec{A}_{ap} = \vec{0}$$

has a non-trivial solution.

So

$$k_1\vec{A}_{a1} + k_2\vec{A}_{a2} + \dots + k_p\vec{A}_{ap} + 0\vec{A}_{a(p+1)} + \dots\dots + 0\vec{A}_{am} = \vec{0}$$

also has a non-trivial solution too, where $\vec{A}_{a(p+1)}, \dots, \vec{A}_{am}$ are the rest of the $(m-p)$ vectors. However, this is a contradiction. Therefore, a subset of linearly independent vectors cannot be linearly dependent.

Prove that if a set of vectors is linearly dependent, then at least one vector can be written as a linear combination of others.

Let $\vec{A}_1, \vec{A}_2, \ldots, \vec{A}_m$ be linearly dependent, then there exists a set of numbers $k_1, \ldots, k_m$ not all of which are zero for the linear combination

$$k_1\vec{A}_1 + k_2\vec{A}_2 + \ldots + k_m\vec{A}_m = \vec{0}.$$

Let $k_p \neq 0$ to give one of the non-zero values of $k_i, i = 1, \ldots, m$, be for $i = p$, then

$$A_p = -\frac{k_2}{k_p}\vec{A}_2 - \ldots - \frac{k_{p-1}}{k_p}\vec{A}_{p-1} - \frac{k_{p+1}}{k_p}\vec{A}_{p+1} - \ldots - \frac{k_m}{k_p}\vec{A}_m.$$

and that proves the theorem.

Prove that if the dimension of a set of vectors is less than the number of vectors in the set, then the set of vectors is linearly dependent.

Can you prove it?

How can vectors be used to write simultaneous linear equations?

If a set of m linear equations with n unknowns is written as

$$a_{11}x_1 + \ldots + a_{1n}x_n = c_1$$
$$a_{21}x_1 + \ldots + a_{2n}x_n = c_2$$
$$\vdots \qquad \vdots$$
$$\vdots \qquad \vdots$$
$$a_{m1}x_1 + \ldots + a_{mn}x_n = c_n$$

where

$x_1, x_2, \ldots, x_n$ are the unknowns, then in the vector notation they can be written as

$$x_1\vec{A}_1 + x_2\vec{A}_2 + \ldots + x_n\vec{A}_n = \vec{C}$$

where

$$\vec{A}_1 = \begin{bmatrix} a_{11} \\ \vdots \\ a_{m1} \end{bmatrix}$$

where

$$\vec{A}_1 = \begin{bmatrix} a_{11} \\ \vdots \\ a_{m1} \end{bmatrix}$$

$$\vec{A}_2 = \begin{bmatrix} a_{12} \\ \vdots \\ a_{m2} \end{bmatrix}$$

$$\vec{A}_n = \begin{bmatrix} a_{1n} \\ \vdots \\ a_{mn} \end{bmatrix}$$

$$\vec{C}_1 = \begin{bmatrix} c_1 \\ \vdots \\ c_m \end{bmatrix}$$

The problem now becomes whether you can find the scalars $x_1, x_2, ..., x_n$ such that the linear combination

$$x_1 \vec{A}_1 + ... + x_n \vec{A}_n = \vec{C}$$

Example 16

Write

$$25x_1 + 5x_2 + x_3 = 106.8$$
$$64x_1 + 8x_2 + x_3 = 177.2$$
$$144x_1 + 12x_2 + x_3 = 279.2$$

as a linear combination of vectors.

Solution

$$\begin{bmatrix} 25x_1 & +5x_2 & +x_3 \\ 64x_1 & +8x_2 & +x_3 \\ 144x_1 & +12x_2 & +x_3 \end{bmatrix} = \begin{bmatrix} 106.8 \\ 177.2 \\ 279.2 \end{bmatrix}$$

$$x_1 \begin{bmatrix} 25 \\ 64 \\ 144 \end{bmatrix} + x_2 \begin{bmatrix} 5 \\ 8 \\ 12 \end{bmatrix} + x_3 \begin{bmatrix} 1 \\ 1 \\ 1 \end{bmatrix} = \begin{bmatrix} 106.8 \\ 177.2 \\ 279.2 \end{bmatrix}$$

What is the definition of the dot product of two vectors?

Let $\vec{A} = [a_1, a_2, ..., a_n]$ and $\vec{B} = [b_1, b_2, ..., b_n]$ be two n-dimensional vectors. Then the dot product of the two vectors $\vec{A}$ and $\vec{B}$ is defined as

$$\vec{A} \cdot \vec{B} = a_1 b_1 + a_2 b_2 + ... + a_n b_n = \sum_{i=1}^{n} a_i b_i$$

A dot product is also called an inner product or scalar.

Example 17

Find the dot product of the two vectors $\vec{A}$ = (4, 1, 2, 3) and $\vec{B}$ = (3, 1, 7, 2).

Solution

$$\vec{A} \cdot \vec{B} = (4,1,2,3) \cdot (3,1,7,2)$$
$$= (4)(3)+(1)(1)+(2)(7)+(3)(2)$$
$$= 33$$

Example 18

A product line needs three types of rubber as given in the table below.

Rubber Type	Weight (lbs)	Cost per pound ($)
A	200	20.23
B	250	30.56
C	310	29.12

Use the definition of a dot product to find the total price of the rubber needed.

Solution

The weight vector is given by
$$\vec{W} = (200,250,310)$$
and the cost vector is given by
$$\vec{C} = (20.23,30.56,29.12).$$

The total cost of the rubber would be the dot product of $\vec{W}$ and $\vec{C}$.

$$\begin{aligned}
\vec{W} \cdot \vec{C} &= (200,250,310) \cdot (20.23,30.56,29.12) \\
&= (200)(20.23) + (250)(30.56) + (310)(29.12) \\
&= 4046 + 7640 + 9027.2 \\
&= \$20713.20
\end{aligned}$$

Key Terms:

Vector
Addition of vectors
Rank
Dot Product
Subtraction of vectors
Unit vector
Scalar multiplication of vectors
Null vector
Linear combination of vectors
Linearly independent vectors

Problem Set

Chapter 04.02
Vectors

1. For

$$\vec{A} = \begin{bmatrix} 2 \\ 9 \\ -7 \end{bmatrix}, \vec{B} = \begin{bmatrix} 3 \\ 2 \\ 5 \end{bmatrix}, \vec{C} = \begin{bmatrix} 1 \\ 1 \\ 1 \end{bmatrix}$$

   find $\vec{A} + \vec{B}$ and $2\vec{A} - 3\vec{B} + \vec{C}$.

2. Are

$$\vec{A} = \begin{bmatrix} 1 \\ 1 \\ 1 \end{bmatrix}, \vec{B} = \begin{bmatrix} 1 \\ 2 \\ 5 \end{bmatrix}, \vec{C} = \begin{bmatrix} 1 \\ 4 \\ 25 \end{bmatrix}$$

   linearly independent?.
   What is the rank of the above set of vectors?
3. Are

$$\vec{A} = \begin{bmatrix} 1 \\ 1 \\ 1 \end{bmatrix}, \vec{B} = \begin{bmatrix} 1 \\ 2 \\ 5 \end{bmatrix}, \vec{C} = \begin{bmatrix} 3 \\ 5 \\ 7 \end{bmatrix}$$

   linearly independent?.
   What is the rank of the above set of vectors?

4. Are

$$\vec{A} = \begin{bmatrix} 1 \\ 2 \\ 5 \end{bmatrix}, \vec{B} = \begin{bmatrix} 2 \\ 4 \\ 10 \end{bmatrix}, \vec{C} = \begin{bmatrix} 1.1 \\ 2.2 \\ 5.5 \end{bmatrix}$$

   linearly independent?
   What is the rank of the above set of vectors?

5. If a set of vectors contains the null vector, the set of
   vectors is linearly
     (A) Independent
     (B) Dependent?

6. If a set of vectors is linearly independent, a subset of the vectors is linearly
     (A) Independent.
     (B) Dependent.

7. If a set of vectors is linearly dependent, then
   (A) At least one vector can be written as a linear combination of others.
   (B) At least one vector is a null vector.

8. If the dimension of a set of vectors is less than the number of vectors in the set, then the set of vectors is linearly
   (A) Dependent.
   (B) Independent.

9. Find the dot product of $\vec{A} = (2,1,2.5,3)$ and $\vec{B} = (-3,2,1,2.5)$

10. If $\vec{u}, \vec{v}, \vec{w}$ are three nonzero vector of 2-dimensions, then
    (A) $\vec{u}, \vec{v}, \vec{w}$ are linearly independent
    (B) $\vec{u}, \vec{v}, \vec{w}$ are linearly dependent
    (C) $\vec{u}, \vec{v}, \vec{w}$ are unit vectors
    (D) $k_1\vec{u} + k_2\vec{v} + k_3\vec{v} = \vec{0}$ has a unique solution.

11. $\vec{u}$ and $\vec{v}$ are two non-zero vectors of dimension n. Prove that if $\vec{u}$ and $\vec{v}$ are linearly dependent, there is a scalar q such that $\vec{v} = q\vec{u}$.

12. $\vec{u}$ and $\vec{v}$ are two non-zero vectors of dimension n. Prove that if there is a scalar q such that $\vec{v} = q\vec{u}$, then $\vec{u}$ and $\vec{v}$ are linearly dependent.

Answers to Selected Problems:

1. $\begin{bmatrix} 5 \\ 11 \\ -2 \end{bmatrix} ; \begin{bmatrix} -4 \\ 13 \\ -28 \end{bmatrix}$

2. 3

3. 3

4. No;1

5. B

6. A

7. A

8. A

9. 6

10. B

11. Hint :

   Start with $k_1\vec{u} + k_2\vec{v} = \vec{0}$

   Show that $k_1 \neq 0$ and $k_2 \neq 0$ because $\vec{u}$ and $\vec{v}$ are both nonzero.

   Hence

   $$\vec{v} = -\frac{k_1}{k_2}\vec{u}$$

   $$= q\vec{u} . \qquad\qquad \left(q = -\frac{k_1}{k_2} \right)$$

12. Hint:

   Since

   $$\vec{v} = q\vec{u}$$

   $$\vec{v} - q\vec{u} = \vec{0}$$

   $q \neq 0$, otherwise $\vec{v} = \vec{0}$

   So the equation

   $$k_1\vec{v} + k_2\vec{u} = \vec{0}$$

has a non trivial solution of
$k_1 = 1, k_2 = q \neq 0$.

Chapter 04.03
Binary Matrix Operations

After reading this chapter, you should be able to
1. *add, subtract, and multiply matrices, and*
2. *apply rules of binary operations on matrices.*

How do you add two matrices?

Two matrices $[A]$ and $[B]$ can be added only if they are the same size. The addition is then shown as

$$[C] = [A] + [B]$$

where

$$c_{ij} = a_{ij} + b_{ij}$$

Example 1

Add the following two matrices.

$$[A] = \begin{bmatrix} 5 & 2 & 3 \\ 1 & 2 & 7 \end{bmatrix} \qquad [B] = \begin{bmatrix} 6 & 7 & -2 \\ 3 & 5 & 19 \end{bmatrix}$$

Solution

$$[C] = [A] + [B]$$

$$= \begin{bmatrix} 5 & 2 & 3 \\ 1 & 2 & 7 \end{bmatrix} + \begin{bmatrix} 6 & 7 & -2 \\ 3 & 5 & 19 \end{bmatrix}$$

$$= \begin{bmatrix} 5+6 & 2+7 & 3-2 \\ 1+3 & 2+5 & 7+19 \end{bmatrix}$$

$$= \begin{bmatrix} 11 & 9 & 1 \\ 4 & 7 & 26 \end{bmatrix}$$

Example 2

Blowout r'us store has two store locations A and B, and their sales of tires are given by make (in rows) and quarters (in columns) as shown below.

04.03.1

$$[A] = \begin{bmatrix} 25 & 20 & 3 & 2 \\ 5 & 10 & 15 & 25 \\ 6 & 16 & 7 & 27 \end{bmatrix}$$

$$[B] = \begin{bmatrix} 20 & 5 & 4 & 0 \\ 3 & 6 & 15 & 21 \\ 4 & 1 & 7 & 20 \end{bmatrix}$$

where the rows represent the sale of Tirestone, Michigan and Copper tires respectively and the columns represent the quarter number: 1, 2, 3 and 4. What are the total tire sales for the two locations by make and quarter?

Solution

$$[C] = [A] + [B]$$

$$= \begin{bmatrix} 25 & 20 & 3 & 2 \\ 5 & 10 & 15 & 25 \\ 6 & 16 & 7 & 27 \end{bmatrix} + \begin{bmatrix} 20 & 5 & 4 & 0 \\ 3 & 6 & 15 & 21 \\ 4 & 1 & 7 & 20 \end{bmatrix}$$

$$= \begin{bmatrix} (25+20) & (20+5) & (3+4) & (2+0) \\ (5+3) & (10+6) & (15+15) & (25+21) \\ (6+4) & (16+1) & (7+7) & (27+20) \end{bmatrix}$$

$$= \begin{bmatrix} 45 & 25 & 7 & 2 \\ 8 & 16 & 30 & 46 \\ 10 & 17 & 14 & 47 \end{bmatrix}$$

So if one wants to know the total number of Copper tires sold in quarter 4 at the two locations, we would look at Row 3 – Column 4 to give $c_{34} = 47$.

How do you subtract two matrices?

Two matrices $[A]$ and $[B]$ can be subtracted only if they are the same size. The subtraction is then given by

$$[D] = [A] - [B]$$

Where

$$d_{ij} = a_{ij} - b_{ij}$$

Example 3

Subtract matrix $[B]$ from matrix $[A]$.

$$[A] = \begin{bmatrix} 5 & 2 & 3 \\ 1 & 2 & 7 \end{bmatrix}$$

$$[B] = \begin{bmatrix} 6 & 7 & -2 \\ 3 & 5 & 19 \end{bmatrix}$$

Solution

$$[D] = [A] - [B]$$

$$= \begin{bmatrix} 5 & 2 & 3 \\ 1 & 2 & 7 \end{bmatrix} - \begin{bmatrix} 6 & 7 & -2 \\ 3 & 5 & 19 \end{bmatrix}$$

$$= \begin{bmatrix} (5-6) & (2-7) & (3-(-2)) \\ (1-3) & (2-5) & (7-19) \end{bmatrix}$$

$$= \begin{bmatrix} -1 & -5 & 5 \\ -2 & -3 & -12 \end{bmatrix}$$

Example 4

Blowout r'us has two store locations A and B and their sales of tires are given by make (in rows) and quarters (in columns) as shown below.

$$[A] = \begin{bmatrix} 25 & 20 & 3 & 2 \\ 5 & 10 & 15 & 25 \\ 6 & 16 & 7 & 27 \end{bmatrix}$$

$$[B] = \begin{bmatrix} 20 & 5 & 4 & 0 \\ 3 & 6 & 15 & 21 \\ 4 & 1 & 7 & 20 \end{bmatrix}$$

where the rows represent the sale of Tirestone, Michigan and Copper tires respectively and the columns represent the quarter number: 1, 2, 3, and 4. How many more tires did store A sell than store B of each brand in each quarter?

Solution

$$[D] = [A] - [B]$$

$$= \begin{bmatrix} 25 & 20 & 3 & 2 \\ 5 & 10 & 15 & 25 \\ 6 & 16 & 7 & 27 \end{bmatrix} - \begin{bmatrix} 20 & 5 & 4 & 0 \\ 3 & 6 & 15 & 21 \\ 4 & 1 & 7 & 20 \end{bmatrix}$$

$$= \begin{bmatrix} 25-20 & 20-5 & 3-4 & 2-0 \\ 5-3 & 10-6 & 15-15 & 25-21 \\ 6-4 & 16-1 & 7-7 & 27-20 \end{bmatrix}$$

$$= \begin{bmatrix} 5 & 15 & -1 & 2 \\ 2 & 4 & 0 & 4 \\ 2 & 15 & 0 & 7 \end{bmatrix}$$

So if you want to know how many more Copper tires were sold in quarter 4 in store A than store B, $d_{34} = 7$. Note that $d_{13} = -1$ implies that store A sold 1 less Michigan tire than store B in quarter 3.

How do I multiply two matrices?

Two matrices $[A]$ and $[B]$ can be multiplied only if the number of columns of $[A]$ is equal to the number of rows of $[B]$ to give

$$[C]_{m\times n} = [A]_{m\times p}[B]_{p\times n}$$

If $[A]$ is a $m\times p$ matrix and $[B]$ is a $p\times n$ matrix, the resulting matrix $[C]$ is a $m\times n$ matrix.

So how does one calculate the elements of $[C]$ matrix?

$$c_{ij} = \sum_{k=1}^{p} a_{ik}b_{kj}$$
$$= a_{i1}b_{1j} + a_{i2}b_{2j} + \ldots\ldots + a_{ip}b_{pj}$$

for each $i = 1, 2,\ldots\ldots, m$ and $j = 1, 2,\ldots\ldots, n$.

To put it in simpler terms, the ith row and j^{th} column of the $[C]$ matrix in $[C] = [A][B]$ is calculated by multiplying the ith row of $[A]$ by the jth column of $[B]$, that is,

$$c_{ij} = \begin{bmatrix} a_{i1} & a_{i2} & \ldots\ldots a_{ip} \end{bmatrix} \begin{bmatrix} b_{1j} \\ b_{2j} \\ \vdots \\ \vdots \\ b_{pj} \end{bmatrix}$$
$$= a_{i1}\,b_{1j} + a_{i2}\,b_{2j} + \ldots\ldots + a_{ip}\,b_{pj}.$$
$$= \sum_{k=1}^{p} a_{ik}b_{kj}$$

Example 5

Given

$$[A] = \begin{bmatrix} 5 & 2 & 3 \\ 1 & 2 & 7 \end{bmatrix}$$

$$[B] = \begin{bmatrix} 3 & -2 \\ 5 & -8 \\ 9 & -10 \end{bmatrix}$$

Find

$$[C] = [A][B]$$

Solution

c_{12} can be found by multiplying the first row of $[A]$ by the second column of $[B]$,

$$c_{12} = \begin{bmatrix} 5 & 2 & 3 \end{bmatrix} \begin{bmatrix} -2 \\ -8 \\ -10 \end{bmatrix}$$

$$= (5)(-2) + (2)(-8) + (3)(-10)$$
$$= -56$$

Similarly, one can find the other elements of [C] to give

$$[C] = \begin{bmatrix} 52 & -56 \\ 76 & -88 \end{bmatrix}$$

Example 6

Blowout r'us store location A and the sales of tires are given by make (in rows) and quarters (in columns) as shown below

$$[A] = \begin{bmatrix} 25 & 20 & 3 & 2 \\ 5 & 10 & 15 & 25 \\ 6 & 16 & 7 & 27 \end{bmatrix}$$

where the rows represent the sale of Tirestone, Michigan and Copper tires respectively and the columns represent the quarter number: 1, 2, 3, and 4. Find the per quarter sales of store A if the following are the prices of each tire.

Tirestone = \$33.25
Michigan = \$40.19
Copper = \$25.03

Solution

The answer is given by multiplying the price matrix by the quantity of sales of store A. The price matrix is $\begin{bmatrix} 33.25 & 40.19 & 25.03 \end{bmatrix}$, so the per quarter sales of store A would be given by

$$[C] = \begin{bmatrix} 33.25 & 40.19 & 25.03 \end{bmatrix} \begin{bmatrix} 25 & 20 & 3 & 2 \\ 5 & 10 & 15 & 25 \\ 6 & 16 & 7 & 27 \end{bmatrix}$$

$$c_{ij} = \sum_{k=1}^{3} a_{ik} b_{kj}$$

$$c_{11} = \sum_{k=1}^{3} a_{1k} b_{k1}$$

$$= a_{11}b_{11} + a_{12}b_{21} + a_{13}b_{31}$$
$$= (33.25)(25) + (40.19)(5) + (25.03)(6)$$
$$= \$1182.38$$

Similarly

$$c_{12} = \$1467.38$$
$$c_{13} = \$877.81$$
$$c_{14} = \$1747.06$$

Therefore, each quarter sales of store A in dollars is given by the four columns of the row vector

$$[C] = \begin{bmatrix} 1182.38 & 1467.38 & 877.81 & 1747.06 \end{bmatrix}$$

Remember since we are multiplying a 1×3 matrix by a 3×4 matrix, the resulting matrix is a 1×4 matrix.

What is the scalar product of a constant and a matrix?

If $[A]$ is a $n \times n$ matrix and k is a real number, then the scalar product of k and $[A]$ is another $n \times n$ matrix $[B]$, where $b_{ij} = k\, a_{ij}$.

Example 7

Let

$$[A] = \begin{bmatrix} 2.1 & 3 & 2 \\ 5 & 1 & 6 \end{bmatrix}$$

Find $2[A]$

Solution

$$
\begin{aligned}
2[A] &= 2\begin{bmatrix} 2.1 & 3 & 2 \\ 5 & 1 & 6 \end{bmatrix} \\
&= \begin{bmatrix} 2\times2.1 & 2\times3 & 2\times2 \\ 2\times5 & 2\times1 & 2\times6 \end{bmatrix} \\
&= \begin{bmatrix} 4.2 & 6 & 4 \\ 10 & 2 & 12 \end{bmatrix}
\end{aligned}
$$

What is a linear combination of matrices?

If $[A_1],[A_2],.....,[A_p]$ are matrices of the same size and $k_1,k_2,.....,k_p$ are scalars, then

$$k_1[A_1] + k_2[A_2] + ...+ k_p[A_p]$$

is called a linear combination of $[A_1],[A_2],.....,[A_p]$

Example 8

If $[A_1] = \begin{bmatrix} 5 & 6 & 2 \\ 3 & 2 & 1 \end{bmatrix}, [A_2] = \begin{bmatrix} 2.1 & 3 & 2 \\ 5 & 1 & 6 \end{bmatrix}, [A_3] = \begin{bmatrix} 0 & 2.2 & 2 \\ 3 & 3.5 & 6 \end{bmatrix}$

then find

$$[A_1] + 2[A_2] - 0.5[A_3]$$

Solution

$$
\begin{aligned}
&[A_1] + 2[A_2] - 0.5[A_3] \\
&= \begin{bmatrix} 5 & 6 & 2 \\ 3 & 2 & 1 \end{bmatrix} + 2\begin{bmatrix} 2.1 & 3 & 2 \\ 5 & 1 & 6 \end{bmatrix} - 0.5\begin{bmatrix} 0 & 2.2 & 2 \\ 3 & 3.5 & 6 \end{bmatrix} \\
&= \begin{bmatrix} 5 & 6 & 2 \\ 3 & 2 & 1 \end{bmatrix} + \begin{bmatrix} 4.2 & 6 & 4 \\ 10 & 2 & 12 \end{bmatrix} - \begin{bmatrix} 0 & 1.1 & 1 \\ 1.5 & 1.75 & 3 \end{bmatrix} \\
&= \begin{bmatrix} 9.2 & 10.9 & 5 \\ 11.5 & 2.25 & 10 \end{bmatrix}
\end{aligned}
$$

What are some of the rules of binary matrix operations?

Commutative law of addition

If $[A]$ and $[B]$ are $m \times n$ matrices, then
$$[A]+[B]=[B]+[A]]$$

Associative law of addition

If [A], [B] and [C] are all $m \times n$ matrices, then
$$[A]+([B]+[C])=([A]+[B])+[C]$$

Associative law of multiplication

If $[A]$, $[B]$ and $[C]$ are $m \times n, n \times p$ and $p \times r$ size matrices, respectively, then
$$[A]([B][C])=([A][B])[C]$$
and the resulting matrix size on both sides of the equation is $m \times r$.

Distributive law

If $[A]$ and $[B]$ are $m \times n$ size matrices, and $[C]$ and $[D]$ are $n \times p$ size matrices
$$[A]([C]+[D])=[A][C]+[A][D]$$
$$([A]+[B])[C]=[A][C]+[B][C]$$
and the resulting matrix size on both sides of the equation is $m \times p$.

Example 9

Illustrate the associative law of multiplication of matrices using

$$[A]=\begin{bmatrix} 1 & 2 \\ 3 & 5 \\ 0 & 2 \end{bmatrix}, \quad [B]=\begin{bmatrix} 2 & 5 \\ 9 & 6 \end{bmatrix}, \quad [C]=\begin{bmatrix} 2 & 1 \\ 3 & 5 \end{bmatrix}$$

Solution

$$[B][C]=$$

$$=\begin{bmatrix} 2 & 5 \\ 9 & 6 \end{bmatrix}\begin{bmatrix} 2 & 1 \\ 3 & 5 \end{bmatrix}$$

$$=\begin{bmatrix} 19 & 27 \\ 36 & 39 \end{bmatrix}$$

$$[A]([B][C])=\begin{bmatrix} 1 & 2 \\ 3 & 5 \\ 0 & 2 \end{bmatrix}\begin{bmatrix} 19 & 27 \\ 36 & 39 \end{bmatrix}$$

$$=\begin{bmatrix} 91 & 105 \\ 237 & 276 \\ 72 & 78 \end{bmatrix}$$

$$[A][B] = \begin{bmatrix} 1 & 2 \\ 3 & 5 \\ 0 & 2 \end{bmatrix} \begin{bmatrix} 2 & 5 \\ 9 & 6 \end{bmatrix}$$

$$= \begin{bmatrix} 20 & 17 \\ 51 & 45 \\ 18 & 12 \end{bmatrix}$$

$$([A][B])[C] = \begin{bmatrix} 20 & 17 \\ 51 & 45 \\ 18 & 12 \end{bmatrix} \begin{bmatrix} 2 & 1 \\ 3 & 5 \end{bmatrix}$$

$$= \begin{bmatrix} 91 & 105 \\ 237 & 276 \\ 72 & 78 \end{bmatrix}$$

The above illustrates the associative law of multiplication of matrices.

Is [A][B] = [B][A]?

If $[A][B]$ exists, number of columns of $[A]$ has to be same as the number of rows of $[B]$ and if $[B][A]$ exists, number of columns of $[B]$ has to be same as the number of rows of $[A]$. Now for $[A][B]=[B][A]$, the resulting matrix from $[A][B]$ and $[B][A]$ has to be of the same size. This is only possible if $[A]$ and $[B]$ are square and are of the same size. Even then in general $[A][B] \neq [B][A]$

Example 10

Determine if
$$[A][B] = [B][A]$$
for the following matrices
$$[A] = \begin{bmatrix} 6 & 3 \\ 2 & 5 \end{bmatrix}, \quad [B] = \begin{bmatrix} -3 & 2 \\ 1 & 5 \end{bmatrix}$$

Solution

$$[A][B] = \begin{bmatrix} 6 & 3 \\ 2 & 5 \end{bmatrix} \begin{bmatrix} -3 & 2 \\ 1 & 5 \end{bmatrix}$$

$$= \begin{bmatrix} -15 & 27 \\ -1 & 29 \end{bmatrix}$$

$$[B][A] = \begin{bmatrix} -3 & 2 \\ 1 & 5 \end{bmatrix} \begin{bmatrix} 6 & 3 \\ 2 & 5 \end{bmatrix}$$

$$= \begin{bmatrix} -14 & 1 \\ 16 & 28 \end{bmatrix}$$

$$[A][B] \neq [B][A]$$

Key Terms:

Addition of matrices
Subtraction of matrices
Multiplication of matrices
Scalar Product of matrices
Linear Combination of Matrices
Rules of Binary Matrix Operation

Problem Set

Chapter 04.03
Binary Matrix Operations

1. For the following matrices

$$[A] = \begin{bmatrix} 3 & 0 \\ -1 & 2 \\ 1 & 1 \end{bmatrix}, [B] = \begin{bmatrix} 4 & -1 \\ 0 & 2 \end{bmatrix}, [C] = \begin{bmatrix} 5 & 2 \\ 3 & 5 \\ 6 & 7 \end{bmatrix}$$

   Find where possible
   (A) $4[A] + 5[C]$
   (B) $[A][B]$
   (C) $[A] = 2[C]$

2. Food orders are taken from two engineering departments for a takeout. The order is tabulated below.
   Food order:

   $$\begin{array}{c} \\ Mechanical \\ Civil \end{array} \begin{array}{ccc} \overset{Chicken}{\underset{Sandwich}{}} & Fries & Drink \\ \begin{bmatrix} 25 & 35 & 25 \\ 21 & 20 & 21 \end{bmatrix} \end{array}$$

   However they have a choice of buying this food from three different restaurants. Their prices for the three food items are tabulated below

   Price Matrix:

   $$\begin{array}{c} Chicken\ Sandwich \\ Fries \\ Drink \end{array} \begin{array}{ccc} McFat & Burcholestrol & \overset{Kentucky}{\underset{Sodium}{}} \\ \begin{bmatrix} 2.42 & 2.38 & 2.46 \\ 0.93 & 0.90 & 0.89 \\ 0.95 & 1.03 & 1.13 \end{bmatrix} \end{array}$$

   Show how much each department will pay for their order at each restaurant. Which restaurant would be more economical to order from for each department?

3. Given

   $$[A] = \begin{bmatrix} 2 & 3 & 5 \\ 6 & 7 & 9 \\ 2 & 1 & 3 \end{bmatrix}$$

   $$[B] = \begin{bmatrix} 3 & 5 \\ 2 & 9 \\ 1 & 6 \end{bmatrix}$$

$$[C] = \begin{bmatrix} 5 & 2 \\ 3 & 9 \\ 7 & 6 \end{bmatrix}$$

Illustrate the distributive law of binary matrix operations

$$[A]([B] + [C]) = [A][B] + [A][C]$$

4. Let $[I]$ be a $n \times n$ identity matrix. Show that $[A][[I] = [I][A] = [A]$ for every $n \times n$ matrix $[A]$.

$$\text{Let } [C]_{n \times n} = [A]_{n \times n} [I]_{n \times n}$$

5. Consider there are only two computer companies in a country. The companies are named *Dude* and *Imac*. Each year, company *Dude* keeps $1/5^{th}$ of its customers, while the rest switch to *Imac*. Each year, *Imac* keeps $1/3^{rd}$ of its customers, while the rest switch to *Dude*. If in 2002, *Dude* has $1/6^{th}$ of the market and *Imac* has $5/6^{th}$ of the market.

   (A) What is the distribution of the customers between the two companies in 2003? Write the answer first as multiplication of two matrices.
   (B) What would be distribution when the market becomes stable?

6. Given

$$[A] = \begin{bmatrix} 12.3 & -12.3 & 10.3 \\ 11.3 & -10.3 & -11.3 \\ 10.3 & -11.3 & -12.3 \end{bmatrix},$$

$$[B] = \begin{bmatrix} 2 & 4 \\ -5 & 6 \\ 11 & -20 \end{bmatrix}$$

   $[A][B]$ matrix size is _____

7. Given

$$[A] = \begin{bmatrix} 12.3 & -12.3 & 10.3 \\ 11.3 & -10.3 & -11.3 \\ 10.3 & -11.3 & -12.3 \end{bmatrix},$$

$$[B] = \begin{bmatrix} 2 & 4 \\ -5 & 6 \\ 11 & -20 \end{bmatrix}$$

   if $[C] = [A][B]$, then $c_{31} =$ _____

Answers to Selected Problems

1.

(A) $= \begin{bmatrix} 37 & 10 \\ 11 & 33 \\ 34 & 39 \end{bmatrix}$

(B) $= \begin{bmatrix} 12 & -3 \\ -4 & 5 \\ 4 & 1 \end{bmatrix}$

(C) $= \begin{bmatrix} -7 & -4 \\ -7 & -8 \\ -11 & -13 \end{bmatrix}$

2. The cost in dollars is 116.80, 116.75, 120.90 for the Mechanical Department at three fast food joints. So BurCholestrol is the cheapest for the Mechanical Department. The cost in dollars is 89.37, 89.61, 93.19 for the Civil Department at three fast food joints. McFat is the cheapest for the Civil Department.

3. $[B]+[C] = \begin{bmatrix} 3 & 5 \\ 2 & 9 \\ 1 & 6 \end{bmatrix} + \begin{bmatrix} 5 & 2 \\ 3 & 9 \\ 7 & 6 \end{bmatrix}$

$= \begin{bmatrix} 8 & 7 \\ 5 & 18 \\ 8 & 12 \end{bmatrix}$

$[A]([B]+[C]) = \begin{bmatrix} 71 & 128 \\ 155 & 276 \\ 45 & 68 \end{bmatrix}$

$[A][B] = \begin{bmatrix} 17 & 67 \\ 41 & 147 \\ 11 & 37 \end{bmatrix}$

$[A][C] = \begin{bmatrix} 54 & 61 \\ 114 & 129 \\ 34 & 31 \end{bmatrix}$

$[A][B]+[A][C] = \begin{bmatrix} 71 & 128 \\ 155 & 276 \\ 45 & 68 \end{bmatrix}$

4. Hint: $c_{ij} = \sum\limits_{p=1}^{n} a_{ip} i_{pj}$

$$= a_{i1}i_{1j} + \ldots\ldots + a_{i,j-1}i_{j-1,j} + a_{ij}i_{jj} + a_{i(j+1)}i_{(j+1)j} + \ldots\ldots + a_{in}i_{nj}$$

Since

$$i_{ij} = 0 \text{ for } i \neq j$$
$$= 1 \text{ for } i = j$$
$$c_{ij} = a_{ij}$$

So $[A] = [A][I]$

Similarly do the other case

$$[I][A] = [A]. \quad \text{Just do it!}$$

5.

(A) At the end of 2002, Dude has

$$\frac{1}{5} \times \frac{1}{6} + \frac{2}{3} \times \frac{5}{6} = 0.589 .$$

Imac has

$$\frac{4}{5} \times \frac{1}{6} + \frac{1}{3} \times \frac{5}{6} = 0.411$$

In matrix form $\begin{bmatrix} \dfrac{1}{5} & \dfrac{2}{3} \\ \dfrac{4}{5} & \dfrac{1}{3} \end{bmatrix} \begin{bmatrix} \dfrac{1}{6} \\ \dfrac{5}{6} \end{bmatrix} = \begin{bmatrix} 0.589 \\ 0.411 \end{bmatrix}$

(B) Stable distribution is [10/22   12/22] (Try to do this part of the problem first by finding the distribution five years from now).

6. 3×2

$$(10.3 \times 2) + ((-5) \times (-11.3)) + (11 \times (-12.3)) = -58.2$$

Chapter 04.04
Unary Matrix Operations

After reading this chapter, you should be able to:
  1. *know what unary operations means,*
  2. *find the transpose of a square matrix and it's relationship to symmetric matrices,*
  3. *find the trace of a matrix, and*
  4. *find the determinant of a matrix by the cofactor method.*

What is the transpose of a matrix?

Let $[A]$ be a $m \times n$ matrix. Then $[B]$ is the transpose of the $[A]$ if $b_{ij} = a_{ji}$ for all i and j. That is, the ith row and the jth column element of $[A]$ is the jth row and i^{th} column element of $[B]$. Note, $[B]$ would be a $n \times m$ matrix. The transpose of $[A]$ is denoted by $[A]^T$.

Example 1

Find the transpose of
$$[A] = \begin{bmatrix} 25 & 20 & 3 & 2 \\ 5 & 10 & 15 & 25 \\ 6 & 16 & 7 & 27 \end{bmatrix}$$

Solution

The transpose of $[A]$ is
$$[A]^T = \begin{bmatrix} 25 & 5 & 6 \\ 20 & 10 & 16 \\ 3 & 15 & 7 \\ 2 & 25 & 27 \end{bmatrix}$$

Note, the transpose of a row vector is a column vector and the transpose of a column vector is a row vector.

Also, note that the transpose of a transpose of a matrix is the matrix itself, that is, $\left([A]^T\right)^T = [A]$. Also, $(A+B)^T = A^T + B^T ; (cA)^T = cA^T$.

What is a symmetric matrix?

A square matrix $[A]$ with real elements where $a_{ij} = a_{ji}$ for $i = 1,2,...,n$ and $j = 1,2,...,n$ is called a symmetric matrix. This is same as, if $[A] = [A]^T$, then $[A]^T$ is a symmetric matrix.

Example 2

Give an example of a symmetric matrix.
Solution

$$[A] = \begin{bmatrix} 21.2 & 3.2 & 6 \\ 3.2 & 21.5 & 8 \\ 6 & 8 & 9.3 \end{bmatrix}$$

is a symmetric matrix as $a_{12} = a_{21} = 3.2$, $a_{13} = a_{31} = 6$ and $a_{23} = a_{32} = 8$.

What is a skew-symmetric matrix?

A $n \times n$ matrix is skew symmetric if $a_{ij} = -a_{ji}$ for $i = 1,...,n$ and $j = 1,...,n$. This is same as

$$[A] = -[A]^T.$$

Example 3

Give an example of a skew-symmetric matrix.
Solution

$$\begin{bmatrix} 0 & 1 & 2 \\ -1 & 0 & -5 \\ -2 & 5 & 0 \end{bmatrix}$$

is skew-symmetric as
$a_{12} = -a_{21} = 1$; $a_{13} = -a_{31} = 2$; $a_{23} = -a_{32} = -5$. Since $a_{ii} = -a_{ii}$ only if $a_{ii} = 0$, all the diagonal elements of a skew-symmetric matrix have to be zero.

What is the trace of a matrix?

The trace of a $n \times n$ matrix $[A]$ is the sum of the diagonal entries of $[A]$, that is,

$$\text{tr}[A] = \sum_{i=1}^{n} a_{ii}$$

Example 4

Find the trace of

$$[A] = \begin{bmatrix} 15 & 6 & 7 \\ 2 & -4 & 2 \\ 3 & 2 & 6 \end{bmatrix}$$

Solution

$$tr[A] = \sum_{i=1}^{3} a_{ii}$$
$$= (15) + (-4) + (6)$$
$$= 17$$

Example 5

The sales of tires are given by make (rows) and quarters (columns) for Blowout r'us store location A, as shown below.

$$[A] = \begin{bmatrix} 25 & 20 & 3 & 2 \\ 5 & 10 & 15 & 25 \\ 6 & 16 & 7 & 27 \end{bmatrix}$$

where the rows represent the sale of Tirestone, Michigan and Copper tires, and the columns represent the quarter number 1, 2, 3, 4.

Find the total yearly revenue of store A if the prices of tires vary by quarters as follows.

$$[B] = \begin{bmatrix} 33.25 & 30.01 & 35.02 & 30.05 \\ 40.19 & 38.02 & 41.03 & 38.23 \\ 25.03 & 22.02 & 27.03 & 22.95 \end{bmatrix}$$

where the rows represent the cost of each tire made by Tirestone, Michigan and Copper, and the columns represent the quarter numbers.

Solution

To find the total tire sales of store A for the whole year, we need to find the sales of each brand of tire for the whole year and then add to find the total sales. To do so, we need to rewrite the price matrix so that the quarters are in rows and the brand names are in the columns, that is, find the transpose of $[B]$.

$$[C] = [B]^{\text{T}}$$

$$= \begin{bmatrix} 33.25 & 30.01 & 35.02 & 30.05 \\ 40.19 & 38.02 & 41.03 & 38.23 \\ 25.03 & 22.02 & 27.03 & 22.95 \end{bmatrix}^{\text{T}}$$

$$[C] = \begin{bmatrix} 33.25 & 40.19 & 25.03 \\ 30.01 & 38.02 & 22.02 \\ 35.02 & 41.03 & 27.03 \\ 30.05 & 38.23 & 22.95 \end{bmatrix}$$

Recognize now that if we find $[A][C]$, we get

$$[D] = [A][C]$$

$$= \begin{bmatrix} 25 & 20 & 3 & 2 \\ 5 & 10 & 15 & 25 \\ 6 & 16 & 7 & 27 \end{bmatrix} \begin{bmatrix} 33.25 & 40.19 & 25.03 \\ 30.01 & 38.02 & 22.02 \\ 35.02 & 41.03 & 27.03 \\ 30.05 & 38.23 & 22.95 \end{bmatrix}$$

$$= \begin{bmatrix} 1597 & 1965 & 1193 \\ 1743 & 2152 & 1325 \\ 1736 & 2169 & 1311 \end{bmatrix}$$

The diagonal elements give the sales of each brand of tire for the whole year, that is

$$d_{11} = \$1597 \quad \text{(Tirestone sales)}$$
$$d_{22} = \$2152 \quad \text{(Michigan sales)}$$
$$d_{33} = \$1311 \quad \text{(Cooper sales)}$$

The total yearly sales of all three brands of tires are

$$\sum_{i=1}^{3} d_{ii} = 1597 + 2152 + 1311$$
$$= \$5060$$

and this is the trace of the matrix $[A]$.

Define the determinant of a matrix.

The determinant of a square matrix is a single unique real number corresponding to a matrix. For a matrix $[A]$, determinant is denoted by $|A|$ or $\det(A)$. So do not use $[A]$ and $|A|$ interchangeably.

For a 2×2 matrix,

$$[A] = \begin{bmatrix} a_{11} & a_{12} \\ a_{21} & a_{22} \end{bmatrix}$$

$$\det(A) = a_{11}a_{22} - a_{12}a_{21}$$

How does one calculate the determinant of any square matrix?

Let $[A]$ be $n \times n$ matrix. The minor of entry a_{ij} is denoted by M_{ij} and is defined as the determinant of the $(n-1 \times (n-1))$ submatrix of $[A]$, where the submatrix is obtained by deleting the ith row and j^{th} column of the matrix $[A]$. The determinant is then given by

$$\det(A) = \sum_{j=1}^{n} (-1)^{i+j} a_{ij} M_{ij} \quad \text{for any } i = 1, 2, \cdots, n$$

or

$$\det(A) = \sum_{i=1}^{n} (-1)^{i+j} a_{ij} M_{ij} \quad \text{for any } j = 1, 2, \cdots, n$$

coupled with that $\det(A) = a_{11}$ for a 1×1 matrix $[A]$, as we can always reduce the determinant of a matrix to determinants of 1×1 matrices. The number $(-1)^{i+j} M_{ij}$ is called the cofactor of a_{ij} and is denoted by c_{ij}. The above equation for the determinant can then be written as

$$\det(A) = \sum_{j=1}^{n} a_{ij} C_{ij} \text{ for any } i = 1, 2, \cdots, n$$

or

$$\det(A) = \sum_{i=1}^{n} a_{ij} C_{ij} \text{ for any } j = 1, 2, \cdots, n$$

The only reason why determinants are not generally calculated using this method is that it becomes computationally intensive. For a $n \times n$ matrix, it requires arithmetic operations proportional to n!.

Example 6

Find the determinant of

$$[A] = \begin{bmatrix} 25 & 5 & 1 \\ 64 & 8 & 1 \\ 144 & 12 & 1 \end{bmatrix}$$

Solution

Method 1:

$$\det(A) = \sum_{j=1}^{3} (-1)^{i+j} a_{ij} M_{ij} \text{ for any } i = 1, 2, 3$$

Let $i = 1$ in the formula

$$\det(A) = \sum_{j=1}^{3} (-1)^{1+j} a_{1j} M_{1j}$$

$$= (-1)^{1+1} a_{11} M_{11} + (-1)^{1+2} a_{12} M_{12} + (-1)^{1+3} a_{13} M_{13}$$

$$= a_{11} M_{11} - a_{12} M_{12} + a_{13} M_{13}$$

$$M_{11} = \begin{vmatrix} 25 & 5 & 1 \\ 64 & 8 & 1 \\ 144 & 12 & 1 \end{vmatrix}$$

$$= \begin{vmatrix} 8 & 1 \\ 12 & 1 \end{vmatrix}$$

$$= -4$$

$$M_{12} = \begin{vmatrix} 25 & 5 & 1 \\ 64 & 8 & 1 \\ 144 & 12 & 1 \end{vmatrix}$$

$$= \begin{vmatrix} 64 & 1 \\ 144 & 1 \end{vmatrix}$$

$$= -80$$

$$M_{13} = \begin{vmatrix} 25 & 5 & 1 \\ 64 & 8 & 1 \\ 144 & 12 & 1 \end{vmatrix}$$

$$= \begin{vmatrix} 64 & 8 \\ 144 & 12 \end{vmatrix}$$

$$= -384$$

$$\det(A) = a_{11}M_{11} - a_{12}M_{12} + a_{13}M_{13}$$
$$= 25(-4) - 5(-80) + 1(-384)$$
$$= -100 + 400 - 384$$
$$= -84$$

Also for $i = 1$,

$$\det(A) = \sum_{j=1}^{3} a_{1j}C_{1j}$$

$$C_{11} = (-1)^{1+1} M_{11}$$
$$= M_{11}$$
$$= -4$$

$$C_{12} = (-1)^{1+2} M_{12}$$
$$= -M_{12}$$
$$= 80$$

$$C_{13} = (-1)^{1+3} M_{13}$$
$$= M_{13}$$
$$= -384$$

$$\det(A) = a_{11}C_{11} + a_{21}C_{21} + a_{31}C_{31}$$
$$= (25)(-4) + (5)(80) + (1)(-384)$$
$$= -100 + 400 - 384$$
$$= -84$$

Method 2:

$$\det(A) = \sum_{i=1}^{3} (-1)^{i+j} a_{ij} M_{ij} \quad \text{for any } j = 1, 2, 3$$

Let $j = 2$ in the formula

$$\det(A) = \sum_{i=1}^{3} (-1)^{i+2} a_{i2} M_{i2}$$

$$= (-1)^{1+2} a_{12}M_{12} + (-1)^{2+2} a_{22}M_{22} + (-1)^{3+2} a_{32}M_{32}$$

$$= -a_{12}M_{12} + a_{22}M_{22} - a_{32}M_{32}$$

$$M_{12} = \begin{vmatrix} 25 & 5 & 1 \\ 64 & 8 & 1 \\ 144 & 12 & 1 \end{vmatrix}$$

$$= \begin{vmatrix} 64 & 1 \\ 144 & 1 \end{vmatrix}$$

$$= -80$$

$$M_{22} = \begin{vmatrix} 25 & 5 & 1 \\ 64 & 8 & 1 \\ 144 & 12 & 1 \end{vmatrix}$$

$$= \begin{vmatrix} 25 & 1 \\ 144 & 1 \end{vmatrix}$$

$$= -119$$

$$M_{32} = \begin{vmatrix} 25 & 5 & 1 \\ 64 & 8 & 1 \\ 144 & 12 & 1 \end{vmatrix}$$

$$= \begin{vmatrix} 25 & 1 \\ 64 & 1 \end{vmatrix}$$

$$= -39$$

$$\det(A) = -a_{12}M_{12} + a_{22}M_{22} - a_{32}M_{32}$$
$$= -5(-80) + 8(-119) - 12(-39)$$
$$= 400 - 952 + 468$$
$$= -84$$

In terms of cofactors for $j = 2$,

$$\det(A) = \sum_{i=1}^{3} a_{i2}C_{i2}$$

$$C_{12} = (-1)^{1+2} M_{12}$$
$$= -M_{12}$$
$$= 80$$

$$C_{22} = (-1)^{2+2} M_{22}$$
$$= M_{22}$$
$$= -119$$

$$C_{32} = (-1)^{3+2} M_{32}$$
$$= -M_{32}$$
$$= 39$$

$$\det(A) = a_{12}C_{12} + a_{22}C_{22} + a_{32}C_{32}$$
$$= (5)(80) + (8)(-119) + (12)(39)$$
$$= 400 - 952 + 468$$

$$= -84$$

Is there a relationship between det(AB), and det(A) and det(B)?

Yes, if $[A]$ and $[B]$ are square matrices of same size, then

$$\det(AB) = \det(A)\det(B)$$

Are there some other theorems that are important in finding the determinant of a square matrix?

Theorem 1: If a row or a column in a $n \times n$ matrix $[A]$ is zero, then $\det(A) = 0$.

Theorem 2: Let $[A]$ be a $n \times n$ matrix. If a row is proportional to another row, then $\det(A) = 0$.

Theorem 3: Let $[A]$ be a $n \times n$ matrix. If a column is proportional to another column, then $\det(A) = 0$.

Theorem 4: Let $[A]$ be a $n \times n$ matrix. If a column or row is multiplied by k to result in matrix k, then $\det(B) = k\det(A)$.

Theorem 5: Let $[A]$ be a $n \times n$ upper or lower triangular matrix, then $\det(B) = \pi\limits_{i=1}^{n} a_{ii}$.

Example 7

What is the determinant of

$$[A] = \begin{bmatrix} 0 & 2 & 6 & 3 \\ 0 & 3 & 7 & 4 \\ 0 & 4 & 9 & 5 \\ 0 & 5 & 2 & 1 \end{bmatrix}$$

Theorem 1

Solution

Since one of the columns (first column in the above example) of $[A]$ is a zero, $\det(A) = 0$.

Example 8

What is the determinant of

$$[A] = \begin{bmatrix} 2 & 1 & 6 & 4 \\ 3 & 2 & 7 & 6 \\ 5 & 4 & 2 & 10 \\ 9 & 5 & 3 & 18 \end{bmatrix}$$

Theorem 3

Solution

$\det(A)$ is zero because the fourth column

$$\begin{bmatrix} 4 \\ 6 \\ 10 \\ 18 \end{bmatrix}$$

is 2 times the first column

$$\begin{bmatrix} 2 \\ 3 \\ 5 \\ 9 \end{bmatrix}$$

Example 9

If the determinant of

$$[A] = \begin{bmatrix} 25 & 5 & 1 \\ 64 & 8 & 1 \\ 144 & 12 & 1 \end{bmatrix}$$

Theorem 4

is -84, then what is the determinant of

$$[B] = \begin{bmatrix} 25 & 10.5 & 1 \\ 64 & 16.8 & 1 \\ 144 & 25.2 & 1 \end{bmatrix}$$

Solution

Since the second column of $[B]$ is 2.1 times the second column of $[A]$

$$\det(B) = 2.1\det(A)$$
$$= (2.1)(-84)$$
$$= -176.4$$

Example 10

Given the determinant of

$$[A] = \begin{bmatrix} 25 & 5 & 1 \\ 64 & 8 & 1 \\ 144 & 12 & 1 \end{bmatrix}$$

is -84, what is the determinant of

$$[B] = \begin{bmatrix} 25 & 5 & 1 \\ 0 & -4.8 & -1.56 \\ 144 & 12 & 1 \end{bmatrix}$$

Solution

Since $[B]$ is simply obtained by subtracting the second row of $[A]$ by 2.56 times the first row of $[A]$,

$$\det(B) = \det(A)$$
$$= -84$$

Example 11

What is the determinant of

$$[A] = \begin{bmatrix} 25 & 5 & 1 \\ 0 & -4.8 & -1.56 \\ 0 & 0 & 0.7 \end{bmatrix}$$

Theorem 5.

Solution

Since $[A]$ is an upper triangular matrix

$$\det(A) = \prod_{i=1}^{3} a_{ii}$$
$$= (a_{11})(a_{22})(a_{33})$$
$$= (25)(-4.8)(0.7)$$
$$= -84$$

Key Terms:

Transpose
Symmetric Matrix
Skew-Symmetric Matrix
Trace of Matrix
Determinant

Problem Set

Chapter 04.04
Unary Matrix Operations

1. Let
$$[A] = \begin{bmatrix} 25 & 3 & 6 \\ 7 & 9 & 2 \end{bmatrix}.$$
   Find $[A]^{\mathrm{T}}$

2. If $[A]$ and $[B]$ are two $n \times n$ symmetric matrices, show that $[A]+[B]$ is also symmetric. Hint: Let $[C] = [A]+[B]$

3. Give an example of a 4×4 symmetric matrix.

4. Give an example of a 4×4 skew-symmetric matrix.

5. What is the trace of

   (A) $$[A] = \begin{bmatrix} 7 & 2 & 3 & 4 \\ -5 & -5 & -5 & -5 \\ 6 & 6 & 7 & 9 \\ -5 & 2 & 3 & 10 \end{bmatrix}$$

   (B) For
   $$[A] = \begin{bmatrix} 10 & -7 & 0 \\ -3 & 2.099 & 6 \\ 5 & -1 & 5 \end{bmatrix}$$
   Find the determinant of $[A]$ using the cofactor method.

6. $\det(3[A])$ of a $n \times n$ matrix is
   (A) $3\det(A)$
   (B) $3\det(A)$
   (C) $3^{n}\det(A)$
   (D) $9\det(A)$

7. For a 5×5 matrix $[A]$, the first row is interchanged with the fifth row, the determinant of the resulting matrix $[B]$ is
   (A) $\det(A)$
   (B) $-\det(A)$

(C) $5\det(A)$

(D) $2\det(A)$

8. $\det\begin{bmatrix} 0 & 1 & 0 & 0 \\ 0 & 0 & 1 & 0 \\ 0 & 0 & 0 & 1 \\ 1 & 0 & 0 & 0 \end{bmatrix}$ is

(A)   0

(B)   1

(C)   −1

(D)   ∞

9.   Without using the cofactor method of finding determinants, find the   determinant of

$$[A] = \begin{bmatrix} 0 & 0 & 0 \\ 2 & 3 & 5 \\ 6 & 9 & 2 \end{bmatrix}$$

10.   Without using the cofactor method of finding determinants,   find the determinant of

$$[A] = \begin{bmatrix} 0 & 0 & 2 & 3 \\ 0 & 2 & 3 & 5 \\ 6 & 7 & 2 & 3 \\ 6.6 & 7.7 & 2.2 & 3.3 \end{bmatrix}$$

11.   Without using the cofactor method of finding determinants, find the determinant of

$$[A] = \begin{bmatrix} 5 & 0 & 0 & 0 \\ 0 & 3 & 0 & 0 \\ 2 & 5 & 6 & 0 \\ 1 & 2 & 3 & 9 \end{bmatrix}$$

12.   Given the matrix

$$[A] = \begin{bmatrix} 125 & 25 & 5 & 1 \\ 512 & 64 & 8 & 1 \\ 1157 & 89 & 13 & 1 \\ 8 & 4 & 2 & 1 \end{bmatrix}$$

and

$\det(A) = -32400$

find the determinant of

(A) $[A] = \begin{bmatrix} 125 & 25 & 5 & 1 \\ 512 & 64 & 8 & 1 \\ 1141 & 81 & 9 & -1 \\ 8 & 4 & 2 & 1 \end{bmatrix}$

(B) $[A] = \begin{bmatrix} 125 & 25 & 1 & 5 \\ 512 & 64 & 1 & 8 \\ 1157 & 89 & 1 & 13 \\ 8 & 4 & 1 & 2 \end{bmatrix}$

(C) $[B] = \begin{bmatrix} 125 & 25 & 5 & 1 \\ 1157 & 89 & 13 & 1 \\ 512 & 64 & 8 & 1 \\ 8 & 4 & 2 & 1 \end{bmatrix}$

(D) $[C] = \begin{bmatrix} 125 & 25 & 5 & 1 \\ 1157 & 89 & 13 & 1 \\ 8 & 4 & 2 & 1 \\ 512 & 64 & 8 & 1 \end{bmatrix}$

(E) $[D] = \begin{bmatrix} 125 & 25 & 5 & 1 \\ 512 & 64 & 8 & 1 \\ 1157 & 89 & 13 & 1 \\ 16 & 8 & 4 & 2 \end{bmatrix}$

13. What is the transpose of
$$[A] = \begin{bmatrix} 25 & 20 & 3 & 2 \\ 5 & 10 & 15 & 25 \\ 6 & 16 & 7 & 27 \end{bmatrix}$$

14. What values of the missing numbers will make this a skew-symmetric matrix?
$$[A] = \begin{bmatrix} 0 & 3 & ? \\ ? & 0 & ? \\ 21 & ? & 0 \end{bmatrix}$$

15. What values of the missing number will make this a symmetric matrix?
$$[A] = \begin{bmatrix} 2 & 3 & ? \\ ? & 6 & 7 \\ 21 & ? & 5 \end{bmatrix}$$

16. Find the determinant of
$$[A] = \begin{bmatrix} 25 & 5 & 1 \\ 64 & 8 & 1 \\ 144 & 12 & 5 \end{bmatrix}$$

17. What is the determinant of an upper triangular matrix $[A]$ that is of order $n \times n$?

18.   Given the determinant of
$$[A] = \begin{bmatrix} 25 & 5 & 1 \\ 64 & 8 & 1 \\ 144 & 12 & a \end{bmatrix}$$
is -564, find a.

19. Why is the determinant of the following matrix zero?
$$[A] = \begin{bmatrix} 0 & 0 & 0 \\ 2 & 3 & 5 \\ 6 & 9 & 2 \end{bmatrix}$$

20. Why is the determinant of the following matrix zero?
$$[A] = \begin{bmatrix} 0 & 0 & 2 & 3 \\ 0 & 2 & 3 & 5 \\ 6 & 7 & 2 & 3 \\ 6.6 & 7.7 & 2.2 & 3.3 \end{bmatrix}$$

21. Show that if $[A][B] = [I]$, where $[A]$, $[B]$ and $[I]$ are matrices of $n \times n$ size and $[I]$ is an identity matrix, then $\det(A) \neq 0$ and $\det(B) \neq 0$.

Answers to Selected Problems

1. $\begin{bmatrix} 25 & 7 \\ 3 & 9 \\ 6 & 2 \end{bmatrix}$

2. $c_{ij} = a_{ij} + b_{ij}$ for all i, j.

   and

   $c_{ji} = a_{ji} + b_{ji}$ for all i, j.

   $c_{ji} = a_{ij} + b_{ij}$ as $[A]$ and $[B]$ are symmetric

   Hence $c_{ji} = c_{ij}$.

3.
4.

5. a) 19
   b) -150.05

6. C

7. A

8. C

9. 0: Can you answer why?

10. 0: Can you answer why?

11. $5 \times 3 \times 6 \times 9 = 810$: Can you answer why?
12. -32400 b) 32400 c) 32400 d) -32400 e) -64800

13. $[A]^T = \begin{bmatrix} 25 & 5 & 6 \\ 20 & 10 & 16 \\ 3 & 15 & 7 \\ 2 & 25 & 27 \end{bmatrix}$

14. $\begin{bmatrix} 0 & 3 & -21 \\ -3 & 0 & 4 \\ 21 & -4 & 0 \end{bmatrix}$

15. $\begin{bmatrix} 2 & 3 & 21 \\ 3 & 6 & 7 \\ 21 & 7 & 5 \end{bmatrix}$

16. The determinant of $[A]$ is

$$25\begin{bmatrix} 8 & 1 \\ 12 & 5 \end{bmatrix} - 5\begin{bmatrix} 64 & 1 \\ 144 & 5 \end{bmatrix} + 1\begin{bmatrix} 64 & 8 \\ 144 & 12 \end{bmatrix}$$

$$= 25(28) - 5(176) + 1(-384)$$

$$= -564$$

17. The determinant of an upper triangular matrix is the product of its diagonal elements, $\prod\limits_{i=1}^{n} a_{ii}$

18. $\det(A) = -120a + 36$

$120a + 36 = 564$

$a = 5$

19. The first row of the matrix is zero, hence, the determinant of the matrix is zero.

20. Row 4 of the matrix is 1.1 times Row 3. Hence, its determinant is zero.

21. We know that $\det(AB) = \det(A)\det(B)$.

$[A][B] = [I]$

$\det(AB) = \det(I)$

$$\det(I) = \prod\limits_{i=1}^{n} a_{ii} = \prod\limits_{i=1}^{n} 1 = 1$$

$\det(A)\det(B) = 1$

Therefore,

$\det(A) \neq 0$ and

$\det(B) \neq 0$.

Chapter 04.05
System of Equations

After reading this chapter, you should be able to:
1. *setup simultaneous linear equations in matrix form and vice-versa,*
2. *understand the concept of the inverse of a matrix,*
3. *know the difference between a consistent and inconsistent system of linear equations, and*
4. *learn that a system of linear equations can have a unique solution, no solution or infinite solutions.*

Matrix algebra is used for solving systems of equations. Can you illustrate this concept?

Matrix algebra is used to solve a system of simultaneous linear equations. In fact, for many mathematical procedures such as the solution to a set of nonlinear equations, interpolation, integration, and differential equations, the solutions reduce to a set of simultaneous linear equations. Let us illustrate with an example for interpolation.

Example 1

The upward velocity of a rocket is given at three different times on the following table.

Table 5.1. Velocity vs. time data for a rocket

Time, t	Velocity, v
(s)	(m/s)
5	106.8
8	177.2
12	279.2

The velocity data is approximated by a polynomial as
$$v(t) = at^2 + bt + c, \quad 5 \le t \le 12.$$

Set up the equations in matrix form to find the coefficients a, b, c of the velocity profile.

Solution

The polynomial is going through three data points $(t_1, v_1), (t_2, v_2),$ and (t_3, v_3) where from table 5.1.

$$t_1 = 5, v_1 = 106.8$$
$$t_2 = 8, v_2 = 177.2$$

04.05.1

$t_3 = 12, v_3 = 279.2$

Requiring that $v(t) = at^2 + bt + c$ passes through the three data points gives

$$v(t_1) = v_1 = at_1^2 + bt_1 + c$$
$$v(t_2) = v_2 = at_2^2 + bt_2 + c$$
$$v(t_3) = v_3 = at_3^2 + bt_3 + c$$

Substituting the data $(t_1, v_1), (t_2, v_2),$ and (t_3, v_3) gives

$$a(5^2) + b(5) + c = 106.8$$
$$a(8^2) + b(8) + c = 177.2$$
$$a(12^2) + b(12) + c = 279.2$$

or

$$25a + 5b + c = 106.8$$
$$64a + 8b + c = 177.2$$
$$144a + 12b + c = 279.2$$

This set of equations can be rewritten in the matrix form as

$$\begin{bmatrix} 25a + & 5b + & c \\ 64a + & 8b + & c \\ 144a + & 12b + & c \end{bmatrix} = \begin{bmatrix} 106.8 \\ 177.2 \\ 279.2 \end{bmatrix}$$

The above equation can be written as a linear combination as follows

$$a\begin{bmatrix} 25 \\ 64 \\ 144 \end{bmatrix} + b\begin{bmatrix} 5 \\ 8 \\ 12 \end{bmatrix} + c\begin{bmatrix} 1 \\ 1 \\ 1 \end{bmatrix} = \begin{bmatrix} 106.8 \\ 177.2 \\ 279.2 \end{bmatrix}$$

and further using matrix multiplication gives

$$\begin{bmatrix} 25 & 5 & 1 \\ 64 & 8 & 1 \\ 144 & 12 & 1 \end{bmatrix} \begin{bmatrix} a \\ b \\ c \end{bmatrix} = \begin{bmatrix} 106.8 \\ 177.2 \\ 279.2 \end{bmatrix}$$

The above is an illustration of why matrix algebra is needed. The complete solution to the set of equations is given later in this chapter.

A general set of m linear equations and n unknowns,

$$a_{11}x_1 + a_{12}x_2 + \cdots\cdots + a_{1n}x_n = c_1$$
$$a_{21}x_1 + a_{22}x_2 + \cdots\cdots + a_{2n}x_n = c_2$$
$$\cdots\cdots\cdots\cdots\cdots\cdots\cdots\cdots\cdots\cdots$$
$$\cdots\cdots\cdots\cdots\cdots\cdots\cdots\cdots\cdots\cdots$$
$$a_{m1}x_1 + a_{m2}x_2 + \cdots\cdots + a_{mn}x_n = c_m$$

can be rewritten in the matrix form as

$$\begin{bmatrix} a_{11} & a_{12} & . & . & a_{1n} \\ a_{21} & a_{22} & . & . & a_{2n} \\ \vdots & & & & \vdots \\ \vdots & & & & \vdots \\ a_{m1} & a_{m2} & . & . & a_{mn} \end{bmatrix} \begin{bmatrix} x_1 \\ x_2 \\ . \\ . \\ x_n \end{bmatrix} = \begin{bmatrix} c_1 \\ c_2 \\ . \\ . \\ c_m \end{bmatrix}$$

Denoting the matrices by $[A]$, $[X]$, and $[C]$, the system of equation is $[A][X]=[C]$, where $[A]$ is called the coefficient matrix, $[C]$ is called the right hand side vector and $[X]$ is called the solution vector.

Sometimes $[A][X]=[C]$ systems of equations are written in the augmented form. That is

$$[A \vdots C] = \begin{bmatrix} a_{11} & a_{12} & \cdots & a_{1n} & \vdots\, c_1 \\ a_{21} & a_{22} & \cdots & a_{2n} & \vdots\, c_2 \\ \vdots & & & \vdots \\ \vdots & & & \vdots \\ a_{m1} & a_{m2} & \cdots & a_{mn} & \vdots\, c_n \end{bmatrix}$$

A system of equations can be consistent or inconsistent. What does that mean?

A system of equations $[A][X]=[C]$ is consistent if there is a solution, and it is inconsistent if there is no solution. However, a consistent system of equations does not mean a unique solution, that is, a consistent system of equations may have a unique solution or infinite solutions (Figure 1).

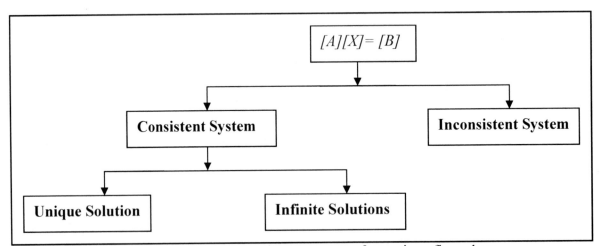

Figure 5.1. Consistent and inconsistent system of equations flow chart.

Example 2

Give examples of consistent and inconsistent system of equations.
Solution

a) The system of equations

$$\begin{bmatrix} 2 & 4 \\ 1 & 3 \end{bmatrix}\begin{bmatrix} x \\ y \end{bmatrix} = \begin{bmatrix} 6 \\ 4 \end{bmatrix}$$

is a consistent system of equations as it has a unique solution, that is,

$$\begin{bmatrix} x \\ y \end{bmatrix} = \begin{bmatrix} 1 \\ 1 \end{bmatrix}.$$

b) The system of equations

$$\begin{bmatrix} 2 & 4 \\ 1 & 2 \end{bmatrix}\begin{bmatrix} x \\ y \end{bmatrix} = \begin{bmatrix} 6 \\ 3 \end{bmatrix}$$

is also a consistent system of equations but it has infinite solutions as given as follows.
Expanding the above set of equations,

$$2x + 4y = 6$$

$$x + 2y = 3$$

you can see that they are the same equation. Hence, any combination of (x, y) that satisfies

$$2x + 4y = 6$$

is a solution.   For example $(x, y) = (1,1)$ is a solution.   Other solutions include
$(x, y) = (0.5, 1.25)$, $(x, y) = (0, 1.5)$, and so on.

c) The system of equations

$$\begin{bmatrix} 2 & 4 \\ 1 & 2 \end{bmatrix}\begin{bmatrix} x \\ y \end{bmatrix} = \begin{bmatrix} 6 \\ 4 \end{bmatrix}$$

is inconsistent as no solution exists.

How can one distinguish between a consistent and inconsistent system of equations?

A system of equations $[A][X] = [C]$ is *consistent* if the rank of A is equal to the rank of the
augmented matrix $[A \vdots C]$
A system of equations $[A][X] = [C]$ is *inconsistent* if the rank of A is less than the rank of
the augmented matrix $[A \vdots C]$.
But, what do you mean by rank of a matrix?
The rank of a matrix is defined as the order of the largest square submatrix whose
determinant is not zero.

Example 3

What is the rank of

$$[A] = \begin{bmatrix} 3 & 1 & 2 \\ 2 & 0 & 5 \\ 1 & 2 & 3 \end{bmatrix}?$$

Solution

The largest square submatrix possible is of order 3 and that is $[A]$ itself. Since
$\det(A) = -23 \neq 0$, the rank of $[A] = 3$.

Example 4

What is the rank of

$$[A] = \begin{bmatrix} 3 & 1 & 2 \\ 2 & 0 & 5 \\ 5 & 1 & 7 \end{bmatrix} ?$$

Solution

The largest square submatrix of $[A]$ is of order 3 and that is $[A]$ itself. Since $\det(A) = 0$, the rank of $[A]$ is less than 3. The next largest square submatrix would be a 2×2 matrix. One of the square submatrices of $[A]$ is

$$[B] = \begin{bmatrix} 3 & 1 \\ 2 & 0 \end{bmatrix}$$

and $\det(B) = -2 \neq 0$. Hence the rank of $[A]$ is 2. There is no need to look at other 2×2 submatrices to establish that the rank of $[A]$ is 2.

Example 5

How do I now use the concept of rank to find if

Step① Find Rank A

$$\begin{bmatrix} 25 & 5 & 1 \\ 64 & 8 & 1 \\ 144 & 12 & 1 \end{bmatrix} \begin{bmatrix} x_1 \\ x_2 \\ x_3 \end{bmatrix} = \begin{bmatrix} 106.8 \\ 177.2 \\ 279.2 \end{bmatrix}$$

is a consistent or inconsistent system of equations?

Solution

The coefficient matrix is

$$[A] = \begin{bmatrix} 25 & 5 & 1 \\ 64 & 8 & 1 \\ 144 & 12 & 1 \end{bmatrix}$$

and the right hand side vector is

$$[C] = \begin{bmatrix} 106.8 \\ 177.2 \\ 279.2 \end{bmatrix}$$

The augmented matrix is

$$[B] = \begin{bmatrix} 25 & 5 & 1 & \vdots & 106.8 \\ 64 & 8 & 1 & \vdots & 177.2 \\ 144 & 12 & 1 & \vdots & 279.2 \end{bmatrix}$$

Since there are no square submatrices of order 4 as $[B]$ is a 3×4 matrix, the rank of $[B]$ is at most 3. So let us look at the square submatrices of $[B]$ of order 3; if any of these square submatrices have determinant not equal to zero, then the rank is 3. For example, a submatrix of the augmented matrix $[B]$ is

$$[D] = \begin{bmatrix} 25 & 5 & 1 \\ 64 & 8 & 1 \\ 144 & 12 & 1 \end{bmatrix}$$

has $\det(D) = -84 \neq 0$.

Hence the rank of the augmented matrix $[B]$ is 3. Since $[A] = [D]$, the rank of $[A]$ is 3. Since the rank of the augmented matrix $[B]$ equals the rank of the coefficient matrix $[A]$, the system of equations is consistent.

Example 6

Use the concept of rank of matrix to find if

$$\begin{bmatrix} 25 & 5 & 1 \\ 64 & 8 & 1 \\ 89 & 13 & 2 \end{bmatrix} \begin{bmatrix} x_1 \\ x_2 \\ x_3 \end{bmatrix} = \begin{bmatrix} 106.8 \\ 177.2 \\ 284.0 \end{bmatrix}$$

is consistent or inconsistent?

Solution

The coefficient matrix is given by

$$[A] = \begin{bmatrix} 25 & 5 & 1 \\ 64 & 8 & 1 \\ 89 & 13 & 2 \end{bmatrix}$$

and the right hand side

$$[C] = \begin{bmatrix} 106.8 \\ 177.2 \\ 284.0 \end{bmatrix}$$

The augmented matrix is

$$[B] = \begin{bmatrix} 25 & 5 & 1 & :106.8 \\ 64 & 8 & 1 & :177.2 \\ 89 & 13 & 2 & :284.0 \end{bmatrix}$$

Since there are no square submatrices of order 4 as $[B]$ is a 4×3 matrix, the rank of the augmented $[B]$ is at most 3. So let us look at square submatrices of the augmented matrix $[B]$ of order 3 and see if any of these have determinants not equal to zero. For example, a square submatrix of the augmented matrix $[B]$ is

$$[D] = \begin{bmatrix} 25 & 5 & 1 \\ 64 & 8 & 1 \\ 89 & 13 & 2 \end{bmatrix}$$

has $\det(D) = 0$. This means, we need to explore other square submatrices of order 3 of the augmented matrix $[B]$ and find their determinants.

That is,

$$[E] = \begin{bmatrix} 5 & 1 & 106.8 \\ 8 & 1 & 177.2 \\ 13 & 2 & 284.0 \end{bmatrix}$$

$\det(E) = 0$

$$[F] = \begin{bmatrix} 25 & 5 & 106.8 \\ 64 & 8 & 177.2 \\ 89 & 13 & 284.0 \end{bmatrix}$$

$\det(F) = 0$

$$[G] = \begin{bmatrix} 25 & 1 & 106.8 \\ 64 & 1 & 177.2 \\ 89 & 2 & 284.0 \end{bmatrix}$$

$\det(G) = 0$

All the square submatrices of order 3×3 of the augmented matrix $[B]$ have a zero determinant. So the rank of the augmented matrix $[B]$ is less than 3. Is the rank of augmented matrix $[B]$ equal to 2?. One of the 2×2 submatrices of the augmented matrix $[B]$ is

$$[H] = \begin{bmatrix} 25 & 5 \\ 64 & 8 \end{bmatrix}$$

and

$$\det(H) = -120 \neq 0$$

So the rank of the augmented matrix $[B]$ is 2.

Now we need to find the rank of the coefficient matrix $[B]$.

$$[A] = \begin{bmatrix} 25 & 5 & 1 \\ 64 & 8 & 1 \\ 89 & 13 & 2 \end{bmatrix}$$

and

$$\det(A) = 0$$

So the rank of the coefficient matrix $[A]$ is less than 3. A square submatrix of the coefficient matrix $[A]$ is

$$[J] = \begin{bmatrix} 5 & 1 \\ 8 & 1 \end{bmatrix}$$

$$\det(J) = -3 \neq 0$$

So the rank of the coefficient matrix $[A]$ is 2.

Hence, rank of the coefficient matrix $[A]$ equals the rank of the augmented matrix $[B]$. So the system of equations $[A][X] = [C]$ is consistent.

Example 7

Use the concept of rank to find if

$$\begin{bmatrix} 25 & 5 & 1 \\ 64 & 8 & 1 \\ 89 & 13 & 2 \end{bmatrix} \begin{bmatrix} x_1 \\ x_2 \\ x_3 \end{bmatrix} = \begin{bmatrix} 106.8 \\ 177.2 \\ 280.0 \end{bmatrix}$$

is consistent or inconsistent.

Solution

The augmented matrix is

$$[B] = \begin{bmatrix} 25 & 5 & 1 & :106.8 \\ 64 & 8 & 1 & :177.2 \\ 89 & 13 & 2 & :280.0 \end{bmatrix}$$

Since there are no square submatrices of order 4×4 as the augmented matrix $[B]$ is a 4×3 matrix, the rank of the augmented matrix $[B]$ is at most 3. So let us look at square submatrices of the augmented matrix (B) of order 3 and see if any of the 3×3 submatrices have a determinant not equal to zero. For example, a square submatrix of order 3×3 of $[B]$

$$[D] = \begin{bmatrix} 25 & 5 & 1 \\ 64 & 8 & 1 \\ 89 & 13 & 2 \end{bmatrix}$$

$\det(D) = 0$

So it means, we need to explore other square submatrices of the augmented matrix $[B]$

$$[E] = \begin{bmatrix} 5 & 1 & 106.8 \\ 8 & 1 & 177.2 \\ 13 & 2 & 280.0 \end{bmatrix}$$

$\det(E0 \neq 12.0 \neq 0$.

So the rank of the augmented matrix $[B]$ is 3.

The rank of the coefficient matrix $[A]$ is 2 from the previous example.

Since the rank of the coefficient matrix $[A]$ is less than the rank of the augmented matrix $[B]$, the system of equations is inconsistent. Hence, no solution exists for $[A][X] = [C]$.

If a solution exists, how do we know whether it is unique?

In a system of equations $[A][X] = [C]$ that is consistent, the rank of the coefficient matrix $[A]$ is the same as the augmented matrix $[A|C]$. If in addition, the rank of the coefficient matrix $[A]$ is same as the number of unknowns, then the solution is unique; if the rank of the coefficient matrix $[A]$ is less than the number of unknowns, then infinite solutions exist.

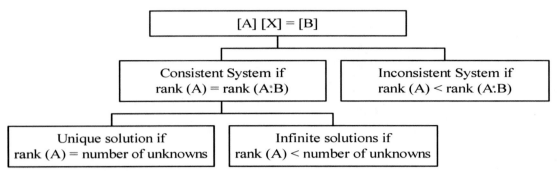

Figure 5.2. Flow chart of conditions for consistent and inconsistent system of equations.

Example 8

We found that the following system of equations

$$\begin{bmatrix} 25 & 5 & 1 \\ 64 & 8 & 1 \\ 144 & 12 & 1 \end{bmatrix} \begin{bmatrix} x_1 \\ x_2 \\ x_3 \end{bmatrix} = \begin{bmatrix} 106.8 \\ 177.2 \\ 279.2 \end{bmatrix}$$

is a consistent system of equations. Does the system of equations have a unique solution or does it have infinite solutions?

Solution

The coefficient matrix is

$$[A] = \begin{bmatrix} 25 & 5 & 1 \\ 64 & 8 & 1 \\ 144 & 12 & 1 \end{bmatrix}$$

and the right hand side is

$$[C] = \begin{bmatrix} 106.8 \\ 177.2 \\ 279.2 \end{bmatrix}$$

While finding out whether the above equations were consistent in an earlier example, we found that the rank of the coefficient matrix (A) equals rank of augmented matrix $[A \colon C]$ equals 3.

The solution is unique as the number of unknowns $= 3 =$ rank of (A).

Example 9

We found that the following system of equations

$$\begin{bmatrix} 25 & 5 & 1 \\ 64 & 8 & 1 \\ 89 & 13 & 2 \end{bmatrix} \begin{bmatrix} x_1 \\ x_2 \\ x_3 \end{bmatrix} = \begin{bmatrix} 106.8 \\ 177.2 \\ 284.0 \end{bmatrix}$$

is a consistent system of equations. Is the solution unique or does it have infinite solutions.

Solution

While finding out whether the above equations were consistent, we found that the rank of the coefficient matrix $[A]$ equals the rank of augmented matrix $(A \colon C)$ equals 2

Since the rank of $[A] = 2 <$ number of unknowns = 3, infinite solutions exist.

If we have more equations than unknowns in [A] [X] = [C], does it mean the system is inconsistent?

No, it depends on the rank of the augmented matrix $[A \colon C]$ and the rank of $[A]$.

a) For example

$$\begin{bmatrix} 25 & 5 & 1 \\ 64 & 8 & 1 \\ 144 & 12 & 1 \\ 89 & 13 & 2 \end{bmatrix} \begin{bmatrix} x_1 \\ x_2 \\ x_3 \end{bmatrix} = \begin{bmatrix} 106.8 \\ 177.2 \\ 279.2 \\ 284.0 \end{bmatrix}$$

is consistent, since

rank of augmented matrix = 3
rank of coefficient matrix = 3

Now since the rank of $(A) = 3 =$ number of unknowns, the solution is not only consistent but also unique.

b) For example

$$\begin{bmatrix} 25 & 5 & 1 \\ 64 & 8 & 1 \\ 144 & 12 & 1 \\ 89 & 13 & 2 \end{bmatrix} \begin{bmatrix} x_1 \\ x_2 \\ x_3 \end{bmatrix} = \begin{bmatrix} 106.8 \\ 177.2 \\ 279.2 \\ 280.0 \end{bmatrix}$$

is inconsistent, since

rank of augmented matrix = 4
rank of coefficient matrix = 3

c) For example

$$\begin{bmatrix} 25 & 5 & 1 \\ 64 & 8 & 1 \\ 50 & 10 & 2 \\ 89 & 13 & 2 \end{bmatrix} \begin{bmatrix} x_1 \\ x_2 \\ x_3 \end{bmatrix} = \begin{bmatrix} 106.8 \\ 177.2 \\ 213.6 \\ 280.0 \end{bmatrix}$$

is consistent, since

rank of augmented matrix = 2
rank of coefficient matrix = 2

But since the rank of $[A] = 2 <$ the number of unknowns = 3, infinite solutions exist.

Consistent systems of equations can only have a unique solution or infinite solutions. Can a system of equations have more than one but not infinite number of solutions?

No, you can only have either a unique solution or infinite solutions. Let us suppose $[A][X] = [C]$ has two solutions $[Y]$ and $[Z]$ so that

$$[A][Y] = [C]$$
$$[A][Z] = [C]$$

If r is a constant, then from the two equations

$$r[A][Y] = r[C]$$
$$(1-r)[A][Z] = (1-r)[C]$$

Adding the above two equations gives

$$r[A][Y] + (1-r)[A][Z] = r[C] + (1-r)[C]$$
$$[A](r[Y] + (1-r)[Z]) = [C]$$

Hence

$$r[Y] + (1-r)[Z]$$

is a solution to

$$[A][X] = [C]$$

Since r is any scalar, there are infinite solutions for $[A][X] = [C]$ of the form

$$r[Y] + (1-r)[Z]$$

Can you divide two matrices?

If $[A][B] = [C]$ is defined, it might seem intuitive that $[A] = \dfrac{[C]}{[B]}$, but matrix division is not

defined like that. However an inverse of a matrix can be defined for certain types of square matrices. The inverse of a square matrix $[A]$, if existing, is denoted by $[A]^{-1}$ such that

$$[A][A]^{-1} = [I] = [A]^{-1}[A]$$

Where $[I]$ is the identity matrix.

In other words, let $[A]$ be a square matrix. If $[B]$ is another square matrix of the same size such that $[B][A] = [I]$, then $[B]$ is the inverse of $[A]$. $[A]$ is then called to be invertible or nonsingular. If $[A]^{-1}$ does not exist, $[A]$ is called noninvertible or singular.

If $[A]$ and $[B]$ are two $n \times n$ matrices such that $[B][A] = [I]$, then these statements are also true

- $[B]$ is the inverse of $[A]$
- $[A]$ is the inverse of $[B]$
- $[A]$ and $[B]$ are both invertible
- $[A][B] = [I]$.
- $[A]$ and $[B]$ are both nonsingular
- all columns of $[A]$ and $[B]$ are linearly independent
- all rows of $[A]$ and $[B]$ are linearly independent.

Example 10

Determine if

$$[B] = \begin{bmatrix} 3 & 2 \\ 5 & 3 \end{bmatrix}$$

is the inverse of

Page - 71

$$[A] = \begin{bmatrix} -3 & 2 \\ 5 & -3 \end{bmatrix}$$

Solution

$$
\begin{aligned}
[B][A] &= \begin{bmatrix} 3 & 2 \\ 5 & 3 \end{bmatrix} \begin{bmatrix} -3 & 2 \\ 5 & -3 \end{bmatrix} \\
&= \begin{bmatrix} 1 & 0 \\ 0 & 1 \end{bmatrix} \\
&= [I]
\end{aligned}
$$

Since

$$[B][A] = [I],$$

$[B]$ is the inverse of $[A]$ and $[A]$ is the inverse of $[B]$.

But, we can also show that

$$
\begin{aligned}
[A][B] &= \begin{bmatrix} -3 & 2 \\ 5 & -3 \end{bmatrix} \begin{bmatrix} 3 & 2 \\ 5 & 3 \end{bmatrix} \\
&= \begin{bmatrix} 1 & 0 \\ 0 & 1 \end{bmatrix} \\
&= [I]
\end{aligned}
$$

to show that $[A]$ is the inverse of $[B]$.

Can I use the concept of the inverse of a matrix to find the solution of a set of equations [A] [X] = [C]?

Yes, if the number of equations is the same as the number of unknowns, the coefficient matrix $[A]$ is a square matrix.

Given

$$[A][X] = [C]$$

Then, if $[A]^{-1}$ exists, multiplying both sides by $[A]^{-1}$.

$$[A]^{-1}[A][X] = [A]^{-1}[C]$$
$$[I][X] = [A]^{-1}[C]$$
$$[X] = [A]^{-1}[C]$$

This implies that if we are able to find $[A]^{-1}$, the solution vector of $[A][X] = [C]$ is simply a multiplication of $[A]^{-1}$ and the right hand side vector, $[C]$.

How do I find the inverse of a matrix?

If $[A]$ is a $n \times n$ matrix, then $[A]^{-1}$ is a $n \times n$ matrix and according to the definition of inverse of a matrix

$$[A][A]^{-1} = [I]$$

Denoting

$$[A] = \begin{bmatrix} a_{11} & a_{12} & \cdot & \cdot & a_{1n} \\ a_{21} & a_{22} & \cdot & \cdot & a_{2n} \\ \cdot & & \cdot & \cdot & \cdot \\ \cdot & & \cdot & \cdot & \cdot \\ a_{n1} & a_{n2} & \cdot & \cdot & a_{nn} \end{bmatrix}$$

$$[A]^{-1} = \begin{bmatrix} a'_{11} & a'_{12} & \cdot & \cdot & a'_{1n} \\ a'_{21} & a'_{22} & \cdot & \cdot & a'_{2n} \\ \cdot & & \cdot & \cdot & \cdot \\ \cdot & & \cdot & \cdot & \cdot \\ a'_{n1} & a'_{n2} & \cdot & \cdot & a'_{nn} \end{bmatrix}$$

$$[I] = \begin{bmatrix} 1 & 0 & \cdot & \cdot & \cdot & 0 \\ 0 & 1 & & & & 0 \\ 0 & & \cdot & & & \cdot \\ \cdot & & & 1 & & \cdot \\ \cdot & & & & \cdot & \cdot \\ 0 & \cdot & \cdot & \cdot & \cdot & 1 \end{bmatrix}$$

Using the definition of matrix multiplication, the first column of the $[A]^{-1}$ matrix can then be found by solving

$$\begin{bmatrix} a_{11} & a_{12} & \cdot & \cdot & a_{1n} \\ a_{21} & a_{22} & \cdot & \cdot & a_{2n} \\ \cdot & \cdot & \cdot & \cdot & \cdot \\ \cdot & \cdot & \cdot & \cdot & \cdot \\ a_{n1} & a_{n2} & \cdot & \cdot & a_{nn} \end{bmatrix} \begin{bmatrix} a'_{11} \\ a'_{21} \\ \cdot \\ \cdot \\ a'_{n1} \end{bmatrix} = \begin{bmatrix} 1 \\ 0 \\ \cdot \\ \cdot \\ 0 \end{bmatrix}$$

Similarly, one can find the other columns of the $[A]^{-1}$ matrix by changing the right hand side accordingly.

Example 11

The upward velocity of the rocket is given by

Table 5.2. Velocity vs time data for a rocket

Time, t (s)	Velocity, v (m/s)
5	106.8
8	177.2
12	279.2

In an earlier example, we wanted to approximate the velocity profile by

$$v(t) = at^2 + bt + c, \quad 5 \le t \le 12$$

We found that the coefficients $a, b,$ and c in $v(t)$ are given by

$$\begin{bmatrix} 25 & 5 & 1 \\ 64 & 8 & 1 \\ 144 & 12 & 1 \end{bmatrix} \begin{bmatrix} a \\ b \\ c \end{bmatrix} = \begin{bmatrix} 106.8 \\ 177.2 \\ 279.2 \end{bmatrix}$$

First, find the inverse of

$$[A] = \begin{bmatrix} 25 & 5 & 1 \\ 64 & 8 & 1 \\ 144 & 12 & 1 \end{bmatrix}$$

and then use the definition of inverse to find the coefficients $a, b,$ and c.

Solution

If

$$[A]^{-1} = \begin{bmatrix} a_{11}' & a_{12}' & a_{13}' \\ a_{21}' & a_{22}' & a_{23}' \\ a_{31}' & a_{32}' & a_{33}' \end{bmatrix}$$

is the inverse of $[A]$, then

$$\begin{bmatrix} 25 & 5 & 1 \\ 64 & 8 & 1 \\ 144 & 12 & 1 \end{bmatrix} \begin{bmatrix} a_{11}' & a_{12}' & a_{13}' \\ a_{21}' & a_{22}' & a_{23}' \\ a_{31}' & a_{32}' & a_{33}' \end{bmatrix} = \begin{bmatrix} 1 & 0 & 0 \\ 0 & 1 & 0 \\ 0 & 0 & 1 \end{bmatrix}$$

gives three sets of equations

$$\begin{bmatrix} 25 & 5 & 1 \\ 64 & 8 & 1 \\ 144 & 12 & 1 \end{bmatrix} \begin{bmatrix} a_{11}' \\ a_{21}' \\ a_{31}' \end{bmatrix} = \begin{bmatrix} 1 \\ 0 \\ 0 \end{bmatrix}$$

$$\begin{bmatrix} 25 & 5 & 1 \\ 64 & 8 & 1 \\ 144 & 12 & 1 \end{bmatrix} \begin{bmatrix} a_{12}' \\ a_{22}' \\ a_{32}' \end{bmatrix} = \begin{bmatrix} 0 \\ 1 \\ 0 \end{bmatrix}$$

$$\begin{bmatrix} 25 & 5 & 1 \\ 64 & 8 & 1 \\ 144 & 12 & 1 \end{bmatrix} \begin{bmatrix} a_{13}' \\ a_{23}' \\ a_{33}' \end{bmatrix} = \begin{bmatrix} 0 \\ 0 \\ 1 \end{bmatrix}$$

Solving the above three sets of equations separately gives

$$\begin{bmatrix} a_{11}' \\ a_{21}' \\ a_{31}' \end{bmatrix} = \begin{bmatrix} 0.04762 \\ -0.9524 \\ 4.571 \end{bmatrix}$$

$$\begin{bmatrix} a_{12}' \\ a_{22}' \\ a_{32}' \end{bmatrix} = \begin{bmatrix} -0.08333 \\ 1.417 \\ -5.000 \end{bmatrix}$$

$$\begin{bmatrix} a'_{13} \\ a'_{23} \\ a'_{33} \end{bmatrix} = \begin{bmatrix} 0.03571 \\ -0.4643 \\ 1.429 \end{bmatrix}$$

Hence

$$[A]^{-1} = \begin{bmatrix} 0.04762 & -0.08333 & 0.03571 \\ -0.9524 & 1.417 & -0.4643 \\ 4.571 & -5.000 & 1.429 \end{bmatrix}$$

Now

$$[A][X] = [C]$$

where

$$[X] = \begin{bmatrix} a \\ b \\ c \end{bmatrix}$$

$$[C] = \begin{bmatrix} 106.8 \\ 177.2 \\ 279.2 \end{bmatrix}$$

Using the definition of $[A]^{-1}$,

$$[A]^{-1}[A][X] = [A]^{-1}[C]$$
$$[X] = [A]^{-1}[C]$$

$$\begin{bmatrix} 0.04762 & -0.08333 & 0.03571 \\ -0.9524 & 1.417 & -0.4643 \\ 4.571 & -5.000 & 1.429 \end{bmatrix} \begin{bmatrix} 106.8 \\ 177.2 \\ 279.2 \end{bmatrix}$$

Hence

$$\begin{bmatrix} a \\ b \\ c \end{bmatrix} = \begin{bmatrix} 0.2905 \\ 19.69 \\ 1.086 \end{bmatrix}$$

So

$$v(t) = 0.2905t^2 + 19.69t + 1.086, \ 5 \le t \le 12$$

Is there another way to find the inverse of a matrix?

For finding the inverse of small matrices, the inverse of an invertible matrix can be found by

$$[A]^{-1} = \frac{1}{\det(A)} adj(A)$$

where

$$adj(A) = \begin{bmatrix} C_{11} & C_{12} & \cdots & C_{1n} \\ C_{21} & C_{22} & & C_{2n} \\ \vdots & & & \\ C_{n1} & C_{n2} & \cdots & C_{nn} \end{bmatrix}^{T}$$

where C_{ij} are the cofactors of a_{ij}. The matrix

$$\begin{bmatrix} C_{11} & C_{12} & \cdots & C_{1n} \\ C_{21} & C_{22} & \cdots & C_{2n} \\ \vdots & & & \vdots \\ C_{n1} & \cdots & \cdots & C_{nn} \end{bmatrix}$$

itself is called the matrix of cofactors from $[A]$. Cofactors are defined in Chapter 4.

Example 12

Find the inverse of

$$[A] = \begin{bmatrix} 25 & 5 & 1 \\ 64 & 8 & 1 \\ 144 & 12 & 1 \end{bmatrix}$$

Solution

From Example 4.6 in Chapter 04.06, we found

$$\det(A) = -84$$

Next we need to find the adjoint of $[A]$. The cofactors of A are found as follows.
The minor of entry a_{11} is

$$M_{11} = \begin{vmatrix} 25 & 5 & 1 \\ 64 & 8 & 1 \\ 144 & 12 & 1 \end{vmatrix}$$

$$= \begin{vmatrix} 8 & 1 \\ 12 & 1 \end{vmatrix}$$

$$= -4$$

The cofactors of entry a_{11} is

$$C_{11} = (-1)^{1+1} M_{11}$$

$$= M_{11}$$

$$= -4$$

The minor of entry a_{12} is

$$M_{12} = \begin{vmatrix} 25 & 5 & 1 \\ 64 & 8 & 1 \\ 144 & 12 & 1 \end{vmatrix}$$

$$= \begin{vmatrix} 64 & 1 \\ 144 & 1 \end{vmatrix}$$

$$= -80$$

The cofactor of entry a_{12} is

$$C_{12} = (-1)^{1+2} M_{12}$$
$$= -M_{12}$$
$$= -(-80)$$
$$= 80$$

Similarly

$$C_{13} = -384$$
$$C_{21} = 7$$
$$C_{22} = -119$$
$$C_{23} = 420$$
$$C_{31} = -3$$
$$C_{32} = 39$$
$$C_{33} = -120$$

Hence the matrix of cofactors of $[A]$ is

$$[C] = \begin{bmatrix} -4 & 80 & -384 \\ 7 & -119 & 420 \\ -3 & 39 & -120 \end{bmatrix}$$

The adjoint of matrix $[A]$ is $[C]^{T}$,

$$adj(A) = [C]^{T}$$
$$= \begin{bmatrix} -4 & 7 & -3 \\ 80 & -119 & 39 \\ -384 & 420 & -120 \end{bmatrix}$$

Hence

$$[A]^{-1} = \frac{1}{det(A)} adj(A)$$

$$= \frac{1}{-84} \begin{bmatrix} -4 & 7 & -3 \\ 80 & -119 & 39 \\ -384 & 420 & -120 \end{bmatrix}$$

$$= \begin{bmatrix} 0.04762 & -0.08333 & 0.03571 \\ -0.9524 & 1.417 & -0.4643 \\ 4.571 & -5.000 & 1.429 \end{bmatrix}$$

If the inverse of a square matrix [A] exists, is it unique?

Yes, the inverse of a square matrix is unique, if it exists. The proof is as follows. Assume that the inverse of $[A]$ is $[B]$ and if this inverse is not unique, then let another inverse of $[A]$ exist called $[C]$.

If $[B]$ is the inverse of $[A]$, then

$$[B][A] = [I]$$

Multiply both sides by $[C]$,

$$[B][A][C] = [I][C]$$
$$[B][A][C] = [C]$$

Since $[C]$ is inverse of $[A]$,

$$[A][C] = [I]$$

Multiply both sides by $[B]$,

$$[B][I] = [C]$$
$$[B] = [C]$$

This shows that $[B]$ and $[C]$ are the same. So the inverse of $[A]$ is unique.

Key Terms:

Consistent system
Inconsistent system
Infinite solutions
Unique solution
Rank
Inverse

Problem Set

Chapter 04.05
System of Equations

1. For a set of equations $[A][X] = [B]$, a unique solution exists if
   - (A) rank (A) = rank $(A \vdots B)$
   - (B) rank (A) = rank $(A \vdots B)$ and rank (A) = number of unknowns
   - (C) rank (A) = rank $(A \vdots B)$ and rank (A) = number of rows of (A).

2. The rank of matrix
$$A = \begin{bmatrix} 4 & 4 & 4 & 4 \\ 4 & 4 & 4 & 4 \\ 4 & 4 & 4 & 4 \\ 4 & 4 & 4 & 4 \end{bmatrix} \text{ is }$$
   - (A) 1
   - (B) 2
   - (C) 3
   - (D) 4

3. A 3×4 matrix can have a rank of at most
   - (A) 3
   - (B) 4
   - (C) 5
   - (D) 12

4. If $[A][X] = [C]$ has a unique solution, where the order of $[A]$ is 3×3, $[X]$ is 3×1, then the rank of $[A]$ is
   - (A) 2
   - (B) 3
   - (C) 4
   - (D) 5

5. Show if the following system of equations is consistent or inconsistent. If they are consistent, determine if the solution would be unique or infinite ones exist.
$$\begin{bmatrix} 1 & 2 & 5 \\ 7 & 3 & 9 \\ 8 & 5 & 14 \end{bmatrix} \begin{bmatrix} x_1 \\ x_2 \\ x_3 \end{bmatrix} = \begin{bmatrix} 8 \\ 19 \\ 27 \end{bmatrix}$$

6. Show if the following system of equations is consistent or inconsistent. If they are consistent, determine if the solution would be unique or infinite ones exist.

$$\begin{bmatrix} 1 & 2 & 5 \\ 7 & 3 & 9 \\ 8 & 5 & 14 \end{bmatrix} \begin{bmatrix} x_1 \\ x_2 \\ x_3 \end{bmatrix} = \begin{bmatrix} 8 \\ 19 \\ 28 \end{bmatrix}$$

7. Show if the following system of equations is consistent or inconsistent. If they are consistent, determine if the solution would be unique or infinite ones exist.

$$\begin{bmatrix} 1 & 2 & 5 \\ 7 & 3 & 9 \\ 8 & 5 & 13 \end{bmatrix} \begin{bmatrix} x_1 \\ x_2 \\ x_3 \end{bmatrix} = \begin{bmatrix} 8 \\ 19 \\ 28 \end{bmatrix}$$

8. The set of equations

$$\begin{bmatrix} 1 & 2 & 5 \\ 7 & 3 & 9 \\ 8 & 5 & 14 \end{bmatrix} \begin{bmatrix} x_1 \\ x_2 \\ x_3 \end{bmatrix} = \begin{bmatrix} 8 \\ 19 \\ 27 \end{bmatrix}$$

has
   (A) Unique solution
   (B) No solution
   (C) Infinite solutions

9. For what values of a will the following equation have

$$x_1 + x_2 + x_3 = 4$$
$$x_3 = 2$$
$$(a^2 - 4)x_1 + x_3 = a - 2$$

   (A) Unique solution
   (B) No solution
   (C) Infinite solutions

10. Find if

$$[A] = \begin{bmatrix} 5 & -2.5 \\ -2 & 3 \end{bmatrix}$$

   and

$$[B] = \begin{bmatrix} 0.3 & 0.25 \\ 0.2 & 0.5 \end{bmatrix}$$

   are inverse of each other.

11. Find if

$$[A] = \begin{bmatrix} 5 & 2.5 \\ 2 & 3 \end{bmatrix}$$

   and

$$[B] = \begin{bmatrix} 0.3 & -0.25 \\ 0.2 & 0.5 \end{bmatrix}$$

are inverse of each other.

12. Find the
    (A) cofactor matrix
    (B) adjoint matrix
    of

$$[A] = \begin{bmatrix} 3 & 4 & 1 \\ 2 & -7 & -1 \\ 8 & 1 & 5 \end{bmatrix}$$

13. Find $[A]^{-1}$ using any method for

$$[A] = \begin{bmatrix} 3 & 4 & 1 \\ 2 & -7 & -1 \\ 8 & 1 & 5 \end{bmatrix}$$

14. Prove that if $[A]$ and $[B]$ are both invertible and are square matrices of same order, then

$$([A][B])^{-1} = [B]^{-1}[A]^{-1}$$

15. What is the inverse of a square diagonal matrix? Does it always exist?

16. $[A]$ and $[B]$ are square matrices. If $[A][B] = [0]$ and $[A]$ is invertible, show $[B] = 0$.

17. If $[A][B][C] = [I]$, where $[A]$, $[B]$ and $[C]$ are of the same size, show that $[B]$ is invertible.

18. Prove if $[B]$ is invertible, $[A][B]^{-1} = [B]^{-1}[A]$ if and only if $[A][B] = [B][A]$

19. For

$$[A] = \begin{bmatrix} 10 & -7 & 0 \\ -3 & 2.099 & 6 \\ 5 & -1 & 5 \end{bmatrix}$$

$$[A]^{-1} = \begin{bmatrix} -0.1099 & -0.2333 & 0.2799 \\ -0.2999 & -0.3332 & 0.3999 \\ 0.04995 & 0.1666 & 6.664 \times 10^{-5} \end{bmatrix}$$

Show

$$\det(A) = \frac{1}{\det(A^{-1})}.$$

20. For what values of a does the linear system have
    $x + y = 2$
    $6x + 6y = a$
    (A) infinite solutions
    (B) unique solution

21. Three kids - Jim, Corey and David receive an inheritance of $2,253,453. The money
    is put in three trusts but is not divided equally to begin with. Corey gets three times
    more than David because Corey made an "A" in Dr. Kaw's class. Each trust is put in
    an interest generating investment. The three trusts of Jim, Corey and David pays an
    interest of 6%, 8%, 11%, respectively. The total interest of all the three trusts
    combined at the end of the first year is $190,740.57. How much money was invested
    in each trust? Set the following as equations in a matrix form. Identify the
    unknowns. Do not solve for the unknowns.

22. What is the rank of
    $$\begin{bmatrix} 1 & 2 & 3 \\ 4 & 6 & 7 \\ 6 & 10 & 13 \end{bmatrix}?$$
    Justify your answer.

23. What is the rank of
    $$\begin{bmatrix} 1 & 2 & 3 & 6 \\ 4 & 6 & 7 & 17 \\ 6 & 10 & 13 & 29 \end{bmatrix}?$$
    Justify your answer.

24. What is the rank of
    $$\begin{bmatrix} 1 & 2 & 3 & 6 \\ 4 & 6 & 7 & 18 \\ 6 & 10 & 13 & 30 \end{bmatrix}?$$
    Justify your answer.

25. How many solutions does the following system of equations have
    $$\begin{bmatrix} 1 & 2 & 3 \\ 4 & 6 & 7 \\ 6 & 10 & 13 \end{bmatrix}\begin{bmatrix} a \\ b \\ c \end{bmatrix} = \begin{bmatrix} 6 \\ 17 \\ 29 \end{bmatrix}?$$

Justify your answer.

26. How many solutions does the following system of equations have

$$\begin{bmatrix} 1 & 2 & 3 \\ 4 & 6 & 7 \\ 6 & 10 & 13 \end{bmatrix} \begin{bmatrix} a \\ b \\ c \end{bmatrix} = \begin{bmatrix} 6 \\ 18 \\ 30 \end{bmatrix} ?$$

Justify your answer.

27. By any scientific method, find the second column of the inverse of

$$\begin{bmatrix} 1 & 2 & 0 \\ 4 & 5 & 0 \\ 0 & 0 & 13 \end{bmatrix}.$$

28. Just write out the inverse of (no need to show any work)

$$\begin{bmatrix} 1 & 0 & 0 & 0 \\ 0 & 2 & 0 & 0 \\ 0 & 0 & 4 & 0 \\ 0 & 0 & 0 & 5 \end{bmatrix}$$

29. Solve $[A][X] = [B]$ for $[X]$ if

$$[A]^{-1} = \begin{bmatrix} 10 & -7 & 0 \\ 2 & 2 & 5 \\ 2 & 0 & 6 \end{bmatrix}$$

and

$$[B] = \begin{bmatrix} 7 \\ 2.5 \\ 6.012 \end{bmatrix}$$

30. Let $[A]$ be a 3×3 matrix. Suppose

$$[X] = \begin{bmatrix} 7 \\ 2.5 \\ 6.012 \end{bmatrix}$$

is a solution to the homogeneous set of equations $[A][X] = [0]$ (the right hand side is a zero vector of order 3×1). Does $[A]$ have an inverse?
Justify your answer.

31. Is the set of vectors

$$\vec{A} = \begin{bmatrix} 1 \\ 1 \\ 1 \end{bmatrix}, \vec{B} = \begin{bmatrix} 1 \\ 2 \\ 5 \end{bmatrix}, \vec{C} = \begin{bmatrix} 1 \\ 4 \\ 25 \end{bmatrix}$$

linearly independent? Justify your answer.

32. What is the rank of the set of vectors

$$\vec{A} = \begin{bmatrix} 1 \\ 1 \\ 1 \end{bmatrix}, \vec{B} = \begin{bmatrix} 1 \\ 2 \\ 5 \end{bmatrix}, \vec{C} = \begin{bmatrix} 1 \\ 3 \\ 6 \end{bmatrix}?$$

Justify your answer.

33. What is the rank of

$$\vec{A} = \begin{bmatrix} 1 \\ 1 \\ 1 \end{bmatrix}, \vec{B} = \begin{bmatrix} 2 \\ 2 \\ 4 \end{bmatrix}, \vec{C} = \begin{bmatrix} 3 \\ 3 \\ 5 \end{bmatrix}?$$

Justify your answer.

Answers to Selected Problems:

1. B

2. A

3. A

4. B

5. Consistent; Infinite solutions

6. Inconsistent

7. Consistent; Unique

8. C

9. If $a \neq +2 \ or - 2,$ then there will be a unique solution
   If $a = +2$ or - 2, then there will be no solution.
   Possibility of infinite solutions does not exist.

10. Yes

11. No

12. $\begin{bmatrix} -34 & -18 & 58 \\ -19 & 7 & 29 \\ 3 & 5 & -29 \end{bmatrix} \begin{bmatrix} -34 & -19 & 3 \\ -18 & 7 & 5 \\ 58 & 29 & -29 \end{bmatrix}$

13. $[A]^{-1} = \begin{bmatrix} 2.931 \times 10^{-1} & 1.638 \times 10^{-1} & -2.586 \times 10^{-2} \\ 1.552 \times 10^{-1} & -6.034 \times 10^{-2} & -4.310 \times 10^{-2} \\ -5.000 \times 10^{-1} & -2.500 \times 10^{-1} & 2.500 \times 10^{-1} \end{bmatrix}$

14. $([A][B])^{-1} = [B]^{-1}[A]^{-1}$

    Let $[C] = [A][B]$

    $[C][B]^{-1} = [A][B][B]^{-1}$
    $= [A][I]$
    $= [A]$

    Again

    $[C] = [A][B]$

$$[A]^{-1}[C] = [A]^{-1}[A][B]$$
$$= [I][B]$$
$$= [B]$$

So

$$[C][B]^{-1} = [A] \qquad\qquad (1)$$
$$[A]^{-1}[C] = [B] \qquad\qquad (2)$$

From (1) and (2)

$$[C][B]^{-1}[A]^{-1}[C] = [A][B]$$
$$[A][B][B]^{-1}[A]^{-1}[A][B] = [A][B]$$
$$[A]^{-1}[A][B][B]^{-1}[A]^{-1}[A][B] = [A^{-1}][A][B]$$
$$[B][B]^{-1}[A^{-1}][A][B] = [B]$$
$$[B^{-1}][B][B]^{-1}[A^{-1}][A][B] = [B]^{-1}[B]$$
$$[B]^{-1}[A^{-1}][A][B] = [I]$$

15. **Hint:** Inverse of a square n×n diagonal matrix $[A]$ is $[A]^{-1} = \begin{bmatrix} \dfrac{1}{a_{11}} & 0 & \cdots & 0 \\ 0 & \dfrac{1}{a_{22}} & \cdots & 0 \\ 0 & & & \vdots \\ \vdots & \cdots & \cdots & \dfrac{1}{a_{nn}} \end{bmatrix}$

So inverse exists only if $a_{ii} \neq 0$ for all i.

16. $$[A][B] = [0]$$
$$[A^{-1}][A][B] = [A]^{-1}[0]$$

17. Hint: $\det(AB) = \det(A)\det(B)$

18. Hint: Multiply by $[B]^{-1}$ on both sides, $[A][B][B]^{-1} = [B]^{-1}[A][B]^{-1}$

19.

20.
    (A)   12
    (B)   not possible

21.   J + C + D = $2,253,453
          C = 3D
          0.06J+0.08C+0.11D = $190,740.57
          In matrix form

$$\begin{bmatrix} 1 & 1 & 1 \\ 0 & 1 & -3 \\ 0.06 & 0.08 & 0.11 \end{bmatrix} \begin{bmatrix} J \\ C \\ D \end{bmatrix} = \begin{bmatrix} 2{,}253{,}453 \\ 0 \\ 190{,}740.57 \end{bmatrix}$$

22. In the above matrix, 2(Row 1) + Row 2 = Row 3. Hence, rank is less than 3. Row 1 and Row 2 are linearly independent. Hence, the rank of the matrix is 2.

23. The determinant of all the 3×3 sub-matrices is zero. Hence, the rank is less than 3. Determinant of

$$\begin{bmatrix} 2 & 3 \\ 6 & 7 \end{bmatrix} = -4 \neq 0.$$

Hence, the rank is 2.

24. In the above matrix, 2(Row 1) + Row 2 = Row 3. Hence, rank is less than 3 as the 3 rows are linearly dependant. Determinant of

$$\begin{bmatrix} 2 & 3 \\ 6 & 7 \end{bmatrix} = -4 \neq 0.$$

Hence, the rank is 2.

25. Rank of A = 2
    Rank of A|C = 2
    Number of unknowns = 3.
    There are infinite solutions since rank of A is less than the number of unknowns.

26. Rank of A = 2
    Rank of A|C = 2
    Number of unknowns = 3.
    There are infinite solutions since rank of A is less than the number of unknowns.

27.
$$\begin{bmatrix} 1 & 2 & 0 \\ 4 & 5 & 0 \\ 0 & 0 & 13 \end{bmatrix} \begin{bmatrix} X & a'_{12} & X \\ X & a'_{22} & X \\ X & a'_{32} & X \end{bmatrix} = \begin{bmatrix} 1 & 0 & 0 \\ 0 & 1 & 0 \\ 0 & 0 & 1 \end{bmatrix}$$

$$a'_{12} + 2a'_{22} = 0$$
$$4a'_{12} + 5a'_{22} = 1$$
$$13a'_{32} = 0$$

Simplifying,

$$\begin{bmatrix} a'_{12} \\ a'_{22} \\ a'_{32} \end{bmatrix} = \begin{bmatrix} 0.667 \\ -0.333 \\ 0 \end{bmatrix}$$

28.

$$\begin{bmatrix} 1 & 0 & 0 & 0 \\ 0 & \dfrac{1}{2} & 0 & 0 \\ 0 & 0 & \dfrac{1}{4} & 0 \\ 0 & 0 & 0 & \dfrac{1}{5} \end{bmatrix}$$

29. $[X] = [A] - 1[B]$

$$= \begin{bmatrix} 10 & -7 & 0 \\ 2 & 2 & 5 \\ 2 & 0 & 6 \end{bmatrix} \begin{bmatrix} 7 \\ 2.5 \\ 6.012 \end{bmatrix}$$

$$= \begin{bmatrix} 52.5 \\ 49.06 \\ 50.072 \end{bmatrix}$$

30. Given

$$[A][X] = [0]$$

If $[A]^{-1}$ exists, then

$$[A]^{-1}[A][X] = [A]^{-1}[0]$$
$$[I][X] = [0]$$
$$[X] = [0]$$

This contradicts the given value of $[X]$. Hence, $[A]^{-1}$ does not exist.

31. The set of vectors are linearly independent.

32. Since, the 3 vectors are linearly independent as proved above, the rank of the 3 vectors is 3.

33. By inspection, $\bar{C} = \vec{A} + \vec{B}$. Hence, the 3 vectors are linearly dependent, and the rank is less than 3. Linear combination of $\vec{A}$ and $\vec{B}$, that is, $K_1\vec{A} + K_2\vec{B} = 0$ has only one solution $K_1 = K_2 = 0$. Therefore, the rank is 2.

Chapter 04.06
Gaussian Elimination

After reading this chapter, you should be able to:

1. *solve a set of simultaneous linear equations using Naïve Gauss elimination,*
2. *learn the pitfalls of the Naïve Gauss elimination method,*
3. *understand the effect of round-off error when solving a set of linear equations with the Naïve Gauss elimination method,*
4. *learn how to modify the Naïve Gauss elimination method to the Gaussian elimination with partial pivoting method to avoid pitfalls of the former method,*
5. *find the determinant of a square matrix using Gaussian elimination, and*
6. *understand the relationship between the determinant of a coefficient matrix and the solution of simultaneous linear equations.*

How is a set of equations solved numerically?

One of the most popular techniques for solving simultaneous linear equations is the Gaussian elimination method. The approach is designed to solve a general set of n equations and n unknowns

$$a_{11}x_1 + a_{12}x_2 + a_{13}x_3 + \ldots + a_{1n}x_n = b_1$$
$$a_{21}x_1 + a_{22}x_2 + a_{23}x_3 + \ldots + a_{2n}x_n = b_2$$
$$\begin{array}{cc} . & . \\ . & . \\ . & . \end{array}$$
$$a_{n1}x_1 + a_{n2}x_2 + a_{n3}x_3 + \ldots + a_{nn}x_n = b_n$$

Gaussian elimination consists of two steps

1. Forward Elimination of Unknowns: In this step, the unknown is eliminated in each equation starting with the first equation. This way, the equations are *reduced* to one equation and one unknown in each equation.
2. Back Substitution: In this step, starting from the last equation, each of the unknowns is found.

Forward Elimination of Unknowns:

In the first step of forward elimination, the first unknown, x_1 is eliminated from all rows below the first row. The first equation is selected as the pivot equation to eliminate x_1. So, to eliminate x_1 in the second equation, one divides the first equation by a_{11} (hence called the pivot element) and then multiplies it by a_{21}. This is the same as multiplying the first equation by a_{21}/a_{11} to give

$$a_{21}x_1 + \frac{a_{21}}{a_{11}}a_{12}x_2 + \ldots + \frac{a_{21}}{a_{11}}a_{1n}x_n = \frac{a_{21}}{a_{11}}b_1$$

Now, this equation can be subtracted from the second equation to give

$$\left(a_{22} - \frac{a_{21}}{a_{11}}a_{12}\right)x_2 + \ldots + \left(a_{2n} - \frac{a_{21}}{a_{11}}a_{1n}\right)x_n = b_2 - \frac{a_{21}}{a_{11}}b_1$$

or

$$a'_{22}x_2 + \ldots + a'_{2n}x_n = b'_2$$

where

$$a'_{22} = a_{22} - \frac{a_{21}}{a_{11}}a_{12}$$

$$\vdots$$

$$a'_{2n} = a_{2n} - \frac{a_{21}}{a_{11}}a_{1n}$$

This procedure of eliminating x_1, is now repeated for the third equation to the nth equation to reduce the set of equations as

$$a_{11}x_1 + a_{12}x_2 + a_{13}x_3 + \ldots + a_{1n}x_n = b_1$$
$$a'_{22}x_2 + a'_{23}x_3 + \ldots + a'_{2n}x_n = b'_2$$
$$a'_{32}x_2 + a'_{33}x_3 + \ldots + a'_{3n}x_n = b'_3$$

$$\begin{matrix} \cdot & & \cdot & & \cdot \\ \cdot & & \cdot & & \cdot \\ \cdot & & \cdot & & \cdot \end{matrix}$$

$$a'_{n2}x_2 + a'_{n3}x_3 + \ldots + a'_{nn}x_n = b'_n$$

This is the end of the first step of forward elimination. Now for the second step of forward elimination, we start with the second equation as the pivot equation and a'_{22} as the pivot element. So, to eliminate x_2 in the third equation, one divides the second equation by a'_{22} (the pivot element) and then multiply it by a'_{32}. This is the same as multiplying the second equation by a'_{32}/a'_{22} and subtracting it from the third equation. This makes the coefficient of x_2 zero in the third equation. The same procedure is now repeated for the fourth equation till the nth equation to give

$$a_{11}x_1 + a_{12}x_2 + a_{13}x_3 + \ldots + a_{1n}x_n = b_1$$
$$a'_{22}x_2 + a'_{23}x_3 + \ldots + a'_{2n}x_n = b'_2$$
$$a''_{33}x_3 + \ldots + a''_{3n}x_n = b''_3$$

$$\begin{matrix} \cdot & & \cdot \\ \cdot & & \cdot \\ \cdot & & \cdot \end{matrix}$$

$$a''_{n3}x_3 + \ldots + a''_{nn}x_n = b''_n$$

The next steps of forward elimination are conducted by using the third equation as a pivot equation and so on. That is, there will be a total of $n-1$ steps of forward elimination. At the end of $n-1$ steps of forward elimination, we get a set of equations that look like

$$a_{11}x_1 + a_{12}x_2 + a_{13}x_3 + \ldots + a_{1n}x_n = b_1$$
$$a'_{22}x_2 + a'_{23}x_3 + \ldots + a'_{2n}x_n = b'_2$$
$$a''_{33}x_3 + \ldots + a''_{3n}x_n = b''_3$$

$$\vdots \qquad \vdots$$

$$a_{nn}^{(n-1)}x_n = b_n^{(n-1)}$$

Back Substitution:

Now the equations are solved starting from the last equation as it has only one unknown.

$$x_n = \frac{b_n^{(n-1)}}{a_{nn}^{(n-1)}}$$

Then the second last equation, that is the $(n-1)^{\text{th}}$ equation, has two unknowns: x_n and x_{n-1}, but x_n is already known. This reduces the $(n-1)^{\text{th}}$ equation also to one unknown. Back substitution hence can be represented for all equations by the formula

$$x_i = \frac{b_i^{(i-1)} - \sum\limits_{j=i+1}^{n} a_{ij}^{(i-1)}x_j}{a_{ii}^{(i-1)}} \qquad \text{for } i = n-1, n-2, \ldots, 1$$

and

$$x_n = \frac{b_n^{(n-1)}}{a_{nn}^{(n-1)}}$$

Example 1

The upward velocity of a rocket is given at three different times in Table 1.

Table 1 Velocity vs. time data.

Time, t (s)	Velocity, v (m/s)
5	106.8
8	177.2
12	279.2

The velocity data is approximated by a polynomial as

$$v(t) = a_1 t^2 + a_2 t + a_3, \qquad 5 \le t \le 12$$

The coefficients a_1, a_2, and a_3 for the above expression are given by

$$\begin{bmatrix} 25 & 5 & 1 \\ 64 & 8 & 1 \\ 144 & 12 & 1 \end{bmatrix} \begin{bmatrix} a_1 \\ a_2 \\ a_3 \end{bmatrix} = \begin{bmatrix} 106.8 \\ 177.2 \\ 279.2 \end{bmatrix}$$

Find the values of a_1, a_2, and a_3 using the Naïve Gauss elimination method. Find the velocity at $t = 6, 7.5, 9, 11$ seconds.

Solution

Forward Elimination of Unknowns

Since there are three equations, there will be two steps of forward elimination of unknowns.

<u>First step</u>

Divide Row 1 by 25 and then multiply it by 64, that is, multiply Row 1 by $64/25 = 2.56$.

$$\begin{bmatrix} 25 & 5 & 1 \end{bmatrix} \qquad \begin{bmatrix} 106.8 \end{bmatrix}) \times 2.56 \text{ gives Row 1 as}$$
$$\begin{bmatrix} 64 & 12.8 & 2.56 \end{bmatrix} \qquad \begin{bmatrix} 273.408 \end{bmatrix}$$

Subtract the result from Row 2

$$\begin{array}{ccc} \begin{bmatrix} 64 & 8 & 1 \end{bmatrix} & \begin{bmatrix} 177.2 \end{bmatrix} \\ - \begin{bmatrix} 64 & 12.8 & 2.56 \end{bmatrix} & \begin{bmatrix} 273.408 \end{bmatrix} \\ \hline 0 \quad -4.8 \quad -1.56 \quad -96.208 \end{array}$$

to get the resulting equations as

$$\begin{bmatrix} 25 & 5 & 1 \\ 0 & -4.8 & -1.56 \\ 144 & 12 & 1 \end{bmatrix} \begin{bmatrix} a_1 \\ a_2 \\ a_3 \end{bmatrix} = \begin{bmatrix} 106.8 \\ -96.208 \\ 279.2 \end{bmatrix}$$

Divide Row 1 by 25 and then multiply it by 144, that is, multiply Row 1 by $144/25 = 5.76$.

$$\begin{bmatrix} 25 & 5 & 1 \end{bmatrix} \qquad \begin{bmatrix} 106.8 \end{bmatrix}) \times 5.76 \text{ gives Row 1 as}$$
$$\begin{bmatrix} 144 & 28.8 & 5.76 \end{bmatrix} \qquad \begin{bmatrix} 615.168 \end{bmatrix}$$

Subtract the result from Row 3

$$\begin{array}{ccc} \begin{bmatrix} 144 & 12 & 1 \end{bmatrix} & \begin{bmatrix} 279.2 \end{bmatrix} \\ - \begin{bmatrix} 144 & 28.8 & 5.76 \end{bmatrix} & \begin{bmatrix} 615.168 \end{bmatrix} \\ \hline 0 \quad -16.8 \quad -4.76 \quad -335.968 \end{array}$$

to get the resulting equations as

$$\begin{bmatrix} 25 & 5 & 1 \\ 0 & -4.8 & -1.56 \\ 0 & -16.8 & -4.76 \end{bmatrix} \begin{bmatrix} a_1 \\ a_2 \\ a_3 \end{bmatrix} = \begin{bmatrix} 106.8 \\ -96.208 \\ -335.968 \end{bmatrix}$$

<u>Second step</u>

We now divide Row 2 by –4.8 and then multiply by –16.8, that is, multiply Row 2 by $-16.8/-4.8 = 3.5$.

$$\begin{bmatrix} 0 & -4.8 & -1.56 \end{bmatrix} \qquad \begin{bmatrix} -96.208 \end{bmatrix}) \times 3.5 \text{ gives Row 2 as}$$
$$\begin{bmatrix} 0 & -16.8 & -5.46 \end{bmatrix} \qquad \begin{bmatrix} -336.728 \end{bmatrix}$$

Subtract the result from Row 3

$$
\begin{array}{cc}
\begin{bmatrix} 0 & -16.8 & -4.76 \end{bmatrix} & \begin{bmatrix} -335.968 \end{bmatrix} \\
- \begin{bmatrix} 0 & -16.8 & -5.46 \end{bmatrix} & \begin{bmatrix} -336.728 \end{bmatrix} \\
\hline
\begin{array}{ccc} 0 & 0 & 0.7 \end{array} & 0.76
\end{array}
$$

to get the resulting equations as

$$
\begin{bmatrix} 25 & 5 & 1 \\ 0 & -4.8 & -1.56 \\ 0 & 0 & 0.7 \end{bmatrix}
\begin{bmatrix} a_1 \\ a_2 \\ a_3 \end{bmatrix} =
\begin{bmatrix} 106.8 \\ -96.208 \\ 0.76 \end{bmatrix}
$$

Back substitution

From the third equation

$$0.7a_3 = 0.76$$

$$a_3 = \frac{0.76}{0.7}$$

$$= 1.08571$$

Substituting the value of a_3 in the second equation,

$$-4.8a_2 - 1.56a_3 = -96.208$$

$$a_2 = \frac{-96.208 + 1.56a_3}{-4.8}$$

$$= \frac{-96.208 + 1.56 \times 1.08571}{-4.8}$$

$$= 19.6905$$

Substituting the value of a_2 and a_3 in the first equation,

$$25a_1 + 5a_2 + a_3 = 106.8$$

$$a_1 = \frac{106.8 - 5a_2 - a_3}{25}$$

$$= \frac{106.8 - 5 \times 19.6905 - 1.08571}{25}$$

$$= 0.290472$$

Hence the solution vector is

$$
\begin{bmatrix} a_1 \\ a_2 \\ a_3 \end{bmatrix} =
\begin{bmatrix} 0.290472 \\ 19.6905 \\ 1.08571 \end{bmatrix}
$$

The polynomial that passes through the three data points is then

$$v(t) = a_1 t^2 + a_2 t + a_3$$

$$= 0.290472 t^2 + 19.6905 t + 1.08571, \ 5 \le t \le 12$$

Since we want to find the velocity at $t = 6, 7.5, 9$ and 11 seconds, we could simply substitute each value of t in $v(t) = 0.290472 t^2 + 19.6905 t + 1.08571$ and find the corresponding velocity. For example, at $t = 6$

$$v(6) = 0.290472(6)^2 + 19.6905(6) + 1.08571$$
$$= 129.686 \text{ m/s}$$

However we could also find all the needed values of velocity at t = 6, 7.5, 9, 11 seconds using matrix multiplication.

$$v(t) = \begin{bmatrix} 0.290472 & 19.6905 & 1.08571 \end{bmatrix} \begin{bmatrix} t^2 \\ t \\ 1 \end{bmatrix}$$

So if we want to find $v(6), v(7.5), v(9), v(11)$, it is given by

$$[v(6)\,v(7.5)\,v(9)\,v(11)] = \begin{bmatrix} 0.290472 & 19.6905 & 1.08571 \end{bmatrix} \begin{bmatrix} 6^2 & 7.5^2 & 9^2 & 11^2 \\ 6 & 7.5 & 9 & 11 \\ 1 & 1 & 1 & 1 \end{bmatrix}$$

$$= \begin{bmatrix} 0.290472 & 19.6905 & 1.08571 \end{bmatrix} \begin{bmatrix} 36 & 56.25 & 81 & 121 \\ 6 & 7.5 & 9 & 11 \\ 1 & 1 & 1 & 1 \end{bmatrix}$$

$$= \begin{bmatrix} 129.686 & 165.104 & 201.828 & 252.828 \end{bmatrix}$$

$v(6) = 129.686 \text{ m/s}$
$v(7.5) = 165.104 \text{ m/s}$
$v(9) = 201.828 \text{ m/s}$
$v(11) = 252.828 \text{ m/s}$

Example 2

Use Naïve Gauss elimination to solve
$$20x_1 + 15x_2 + 10x_3 = 45$$
$$-3x_1 - 2.249x_2 + 7x_3 = 1.751$$
$$5x_1 + x_2 + 3x_3 = 9$$
Use six significant digits with chopping in your calculations.
Solution

Working in the matrix form
$$\begin{bmatrix} 20 & 15 & 10 \\ -3 & -2.249 & 7 \\ 5 & 1 & 3 \end{bmatrix} \begin{bmatrix} x_1 \\ x_2 \\ x_3 \end{bmatrix} = \begin{bmatrix} 45 \\ 1.751 \\ 9 \end{bmatrix}$$

Forward Elimination of Unknowns

First step
Divide Row 1 by 20 and then multiply it by –3, that is, multiply Row 1 by $-3/20 = -0.15$.
$([20 \quad 15 \quad 10] \quad [45]) \times -0.15$ gives Row 1 as
$$[-3 \quad -2.25 \quad -1.5] \quad [-6.75]$$

Subtract the result from Row 2

$$\begin{array}{ccc}[-3 & -2.249 & 7] \end{array} \quad [1.751]$$
$$-\begin{array}{ccc}[-3 & -2.25 & -1.5] \end{array} \quad [-6.75]$$
$$\begin{array}{cccc}\hline 0 & 0.001 & 8.5 & 8.501 \end{array}$$

to get the resulting equations as

$$\begin{bmatrix} 20 & 15 & 10 \\ 0 & 0.001 & 8.5 \\ 5 & 1 & 3 \end{bmatrix} \begin{bmatrix} x_1 \\ x_2 \\ x_3 \end{bmatrix} = \begin{bmatrix} 45 \\ 8.501 \\ 9 \end{bmatrix}$$

Divide Row 1 by 20 and then multiply it by 5, that is, multiply Row 1 by $5/20 = 0.25$

$$([20 \quad 15 \quad 10] \quad [45]) \times 0.25 \text{ gives Row 1 as}$$
$$[5 \quad 3.75 \quad 2.5] \quad [11.25]$$

Subtract the result from Row 3

$$\begin{array}{ccc}[5 & 1 & 3] \end{array} \quad [9]$$
$$-\begin{array}{ccc}[5 & 3.75 & 2.5] \end{array} \quad [11.25]$$
$$\begin{array}{cccc}\hline 0 & -2.75 & 0.5 & -2.25 \end{array}$$

to get the resulting equations as

$$\begin{bmatrix} 20 & 15 & 10 \\ 0 & 0.001 & 8.5 \\ 0 & -2.75 & 0.5 \end{bmatrix} \begin{bmatrix} x_1 \\ x_2 \\ x_3 \end{bmatrix} = \begin{bmatrix} 45 \\ 8.501 \\ -2.25 \end{bmatrix}$$

<u>Second step</u>
Now for the second step of forward elimination, we will use Row 2 as the pivot equation and eliminate Row 3: Column 2.
Divide Row 2 by 0.001 and then multiply it by –2.75, that is, multiply Row 2 by $-2.75/0.001 = -2750$.

$$([0 \quad 0.001 \quad 8.5] \quad [8.501]) \times -2750 \text{ gives Row 2 as}$$
$$[0 \quad -2.75 \quad -23375] \quad [-23377.75]$$

Rewriting within 6 significant digits with chopping

$$[0 \quad -2.75 \quad -23375] \quad [-23377.7]$$

Subtract the result from Row 3

$$\begin{array}{ccc}[0 & -2.75 & 0.5] \end{array} \quad [-2.25]$$
$$-\begin{array}{ccc}[0 & -2.75 & -23375] \end{array} \quad [-23377.7]$$
$$\begin{array}{cccc}\hline 0 & 0 & 23375.5 & 23375.45 \end{array}$$

Rewriting within 6 significant digits with chopping

$$[0 \quad 0 \quad 23375.5] \quad [-23375.4]$$

to get the resulting equations as

$$\begin{bmatrix} 20 & 15 & 10 \\ 0 & 0.001 & 8.5 \\ 0 & 0 & 23375.5 \end{bmatrix} \begin{bmatrix} x_1 \\ x_2 \\ x_3 \end{bmatrix} = \begin{bmatrix} 45 \\ 8.501 \\ 23375.4 \end{bmatrix}$$

This is the end of the forward elimination steps.

Back substitution

We can now solve the above equations by back substitution. From the third equation,

$$23375.5x_3 = 23375.4$$

$$x_3 = \frac{23375.4}{23375.5}$$

$$= 0.999995$$

Substituting the value of x_3 in the second equation

$$0.001x_2 + 8.5x_3 = 8.501$$

$$x_2 = \frac{8.501 - 8.5x_3}{0.001}$$

$$= \frac{8.501 - 8.5 \times 0.999995}{0.001}$$

$$= \frac{8.501 - 8.49995}{0.001}$$

$$= \frac{0.00105}{0.001}$$

$$= 1.05$$

Substituting the value of x_3 and x_2 in the first equation,

$$20x_1 + 15x_2 + 10x_3 = 45$$

$$x_1 = \frac{45 - 15x_2 - 10x_3}{20}$$

$$= \frac{45 - 15 \times 1.05 - 10 \times 0.999995}{20}$$

$$= \frac{45 - 15.75 - 9.99995}{20}$$

$$= \frac{29.25 - 9.99995}{20}$$

$$= \frac{19.2500}{20}$$

$$= 0.9625$$

Hence the solution is

$$[X] = \begin{bmatrix} x_1 \\ x_2 \\ x_3 \end{bmatrix}$$

$$= \begin{bmatrix} 0.9625 \\ 1.05 \\ 0.999995 \end{bmatrix}$$

Compare this with the exact solution of

$$[X] = \begin{bmatrix} x_1 \\ x_2 \\ x_3 \end{bmatrix}$$

$$= \begin{bmatrix} 1 \\ 1 \\ 1 \end{bmatrix}$$

Are there any pitfalls of the Naïve Gauss elimination method?

Yes, there are two pitfalls of the Naïve Gauss elimination method.
Division by zero: It is possible for division by zero to occur during the beginning of the $n-1$ steps of forward elimination.
For example

$$5x_2 + 6x_3 = 11$$
$$4x_1 + 5x_2 + 7x_3 = 16$$
$$9x_1 + 2x_2 + 3x_3 = 15$$

will result in division by zero in the first step of forward elimination as the coefficient of x_1 in the first equation is zero as is evident when we write the equations in matrix form.

$$\begin{bmatrix} 0 & 5 & 6 \\ 4 & 5 & 7 \\ 9 & 2 & 3 \end{bmatrix} \begin{bmatrix} x_1 \\ x_2 \\ x_3 \end{bmatrix} = \begin{bmatrix} 11 \\ 16 \\ 15 \end{bmatrix}$$

But what about the equations below: Is division by zero a problem?

$$5x_1 + 6x_2 + 7x_3 = 18$$
$$10x_1 + 12x_2 + 3x_3 = 25$$
$$20x_1 + 17x_2 + 19x_3 = 56$$

Written in matrix form,

$$\begin{bmatrix} 5 & 6 & 7 \\ 10 & 12 & 3 \\ 20 & 17 & 19 \end{bmatrix} \begin{bmatrix} x_1 \\ x_2 \\ x_3 \end{bmatrix} = \begin{bmatrix} 18 \\ 25 \\ 56 \end{bmatrix}$$

there is no issue of division by zero in the first step of forward elimination. The pivot element is the coefficient of x_1 in the first equation, 5, and that is a non-zero number. However, at the end of the first step of forward elimination, we get the following equations in matrix form

$$\begin{bmatrix} 5 & 6 & 7 \\ 0 & 0 & -11 \\ 0 & -7 & -9 \end{bmatrix} \begin{bmatrix} x_1 \\ x_2 \\ x_3 \end{bmatrix} = \begin{bmatrix} 18 \\ -11 \\ -16 \end{bmatrix}$$

Now at the beginning of the 2nd step of forward elimination, the coefficient of x_2 in Equation 2 would be used as the pivot element. That element is zero and hence would create the division by zero problem.

So it is important to consider that the possibility of division by zero can occur at the beginning of any step of forward elimination.

Round-off error: The Naïve Gauss elimination method is prone to round-off errors. This is true when there are large numbers of equations as errors propagate. Also, if there is subtraction of numbers from each other, it may create large errors. See the example below.

Example 3

Remember Example 2 where we used Naïve Gauss elimination to solve
$$20x_1 + 15x_2 + 10x_3 = 45$$
$$-3x_1 - 2.249x_2 + 7x_3 = 1.751$$
$$5x_1 + x_2 + 3x_3 = 9$$
using six significant digits with chopping in your calculations? Repeat the problem, but now use five significant digits with chopping in your calculations.
Solution

Writing in the matrix form
$$\begin{bmatrix} 20 & 15 & 10 \\ -3 & -2.249 & 7 \\ 5 & 1 & 3 \end{bmatrix} \begin{bmatrix} x_1 \\ x_2 \\ x_3 \end{bmatrix} = \begin{bmatrix} 45 \\ 1.751 \\ 9 \end{bmatrix}$$
Forward Elimination of Unknowns

First step
Divide Row 1 by 20 and then multiply it by –3, that is, multiply Row 1 by $-3/20 = -0.15$.
$$([20 \quad 15 \quad 10] \quad [45]) \times -0.15 \text{ gives Row 1 as}$$
$$[-3 \quad -2.25 \quad -1.5] \quad [-6.75]$$
Subtract the result from Row 2
$$\begin{array}{cccc} [-3 & -2.249 & 7] & [1.751] \\ - [-3 & -2.25 & -1.5] & [-6.75] \\ \hline 0 & 0.001 & 8.5 & 8.501 \end{array}$$
to get the resulting equations as
$$\begin{bmatrix} 20 & 15 & 10 \\ 0 & 0.001 & 8.5 \\ 5 & 1 & 3 \end{bmatrix} \begin{bmatrix} x_1 \\ x_2 \\ x_3 \end{bmatrix} = \begin{bmatrix} 45 \\ 8.501 \\ 9 \end{bmatrix}$$
Divide Row 1 by 20 and then multiply it by 5, that is, multiply Row 1 by $5/20 = 0.25$.
$$([20 \quad 15 \quad 10] \quad [45]) \times 0.25 \text{ gives Row 1 as}$$
$$[5 \quad 3.75 \quad 2.5] \quad [11.25]$$
Subtract the result from Row 3
$$\begin{array}{cccc} [5 & 1 & 3] & [9] \\ - [5 & 3.75 & 2.5] & [11.25] \\ \hline 0 & -2.75 & 0.5 & -2.25 \end{array}$$

to get the resulting equations as

$$\begin{bmatrix} 20 & 15 & 10 \\ 0 & 0.001 & 8.5 \\ 0 & -2.75 & 0.5 \end{bmatrix} \begin{bmatrix} x_1 \\ x_2 \\ x_3 \end{bmatrix} = \begin{bmatrix} 45 \\ 8.501 \\ -2.25 \end{bmatrix}$$

Second step

Now for the second step of forward elimination, we will use Row 2 as the pivot equation and eliminate Row 3: Column 2.

Divide Row 2 by 0.001 and then multiply it by –2.75, that is, multiply Row 2 by $-2.75/0.001 = -2750$.

$([0 \quad 0.001 \quad 8.5] \quad [8.501]) \times -2750$ gives Row 2 as

$[0 \quad -2.75 \quad -23375] \quad [-23377.75]$

Rewriting within 5 significant digits with chopping

$[0 \quad -2.75 \quad -23375] \quad [-23377]$

Subtract the result from Row 3

$$\begin{array}{rrr} [0 & -2.75 & 0.5] \quad [-2.25] \\ - [0 & -2.75 & -23375] \quad [-23377] \\ \hline 0 & 0 & 23375 \quad 23374 \end{array}$$

Rewriting within 6 significant digits with chopping

$[0 \quad 0 \quad 23375] \quad [-23374]$

to get the resulting equations as

$$\begin{bmatrix} 20 & 15 & 10 \\ 0 & 0.001 & 8.5 \\ 0 & 0 & 23375 \end{bmatrix} \begin{bmatrix} x_1 \\ x_2 \\ x_3 \end{bmatrix} = \begin{bmatrix} 45 \\ 8.501 \\ 23374 \end{bmatrix}$$

This is the end of the forward elimination steps.

Back substitution

We can now solve the above equations by back substitution. From the third equation,

$$23375x_3 = 23374$$

$$x_3 = \frac{23374}{23375}$$

$$= 0.99995$$

Substituting the value of x_3 in the second equation

$$0.001x_2 + 8.5x_3 = 8.501$$

$$x_2 = \frac{8.501 - 8.5x_3}{0.001}$$

$$= \frac{8.501 - 8.5 \times 0.99995}{0.001}$$

$$= \frac{8.501 - 8.499575}{0.001}$$

$$= \frac{8.501 - 8.4995}{0.001}$$

$$= \frac{0.0015}{0.001}$$

$$= 1.5$$

Substituting the value of x_3 and x_2 in the first equation,

$$20x_1 + 15x_2 + 10x_3 = 45$$

$$x_1 = \frac{45 - 15\,x_2 - 10x_3}{20}$$

$$= \frac{45 - 15 \times 1.5 - 10 \times 0.99995}{20}$$

$$= \frac{45 - 22.5 - 9.9995}{20}$$

$$= \frac{22.5 - 9.9995}{20}$$

$$= \frac{12.5005}{20}$$

$$= \frac{12.500}{20}$$

$$= 0.625$$

Hence the solution is

$$[X] = \begin{bmatrix} x_1 \\ x_2 \\ x_3 \end{bmatrix}$$

$$= \begin{bmatrix} 0.625 \\ 1.5 \\ 0.99995 \end{bmatrix}$$

Compare this with the exact solution of

$$[X] = \begin{bmatrix} x_1 \\ x_2 \\ x_3 \end{bmatrix} = \begin{bmatrix} 1 \\ 1 \\ 1 \end{bmatrix}$$

What are some techniques for improving the Naïve Gauss elimination method?

As seen in Example 3, round off errors were large when five significant digits were used as opposed to six significant digits. One method of decreasing the round-off error would be to use more significant digits, that is, use double or quad precision for representing the numbers. However, this would not avoid possible division by zero errors in the Naïve Gauss elimination method. To avoid division by zero as well as reduce (not eliminate) round-off error, Gaussian elimination with partial pivoting is the method of choice.

How does Gaussian elimination with partial pivoting differ from Naïve Gauss elimination?

The two methods are the same, except in the beginning of each step of forward elimination, a row switching is done based on the following criterion. If there are n equations, then there are $n-1$ forward elimination steps. At the beginning of the kth step of forward elimination, one finds the maximum of

$$\left|a_{kk}\right|, \left|a_{k+1,k}\right|, \ldots\ldots\ldots\ldots, \left|a_{nk}\right|$$

Then if the maximum of these values is $\left|a_{pk}\right|$ in the pth row, $k \leq p \leq n$, then switch rows p and k.

The other steps of forward elimination are the same as the Naïve Gauss elimination method. The back substitution steps stay exactly the same as the Naïve Gauss elimination method.

Example 4

In the previous two examples, we used Naïve Gauss elimination to solve

$$20x_1 + 15x_2 + 10x_3 = 45$$
$$-3x_1 - 2.249x_2 + 7x_3 = 1.751$$
$$5x_1 + x_2 + 3x_3 = 9$$

using five and six significant digits with chopping in the calculations. Using five significant digits with chopping, the solution found was

$$[X] = \begin{bmatrix} x_1 \\ x_2 \\ x_3 \end{bmatrix}$$

$$= \begin{bmatrix} 0.625 \\ 1.5 \\ 0.99995 \end{bmatrix}$$

This is different from the exact solution of

$$[X] = \begin{bmatrix} x_1 \\ x_2 \\ x_3 \end{bmatrix}$$

$$= \begin{bmatrix} 1 \\ 1 \\ 1 \end{bmatrix}$$

Find the solution using Gaussian elimination with partial pivoting using five significant digits with chopping in your calculations.

Solution

$$\begin{bmatrix} 20 & 15 & 10 \\ -3 & -2.249 & 7 \\ 5 & 1 & 3 \end{bmatrix} \begin{bmatrix} x_1 \\ x_2 \\ x_3 \end{bmatrix} = \begin{bmatrix} 45 \\ 1.751 \\ 9 \end{bmatrix}$$

Forward Elimination of Unknowns

Now for the first step of forward elimination, the absolute value of the first column elements below Row 1 is

$$\left|20\right|, \left|-3\right|, \left|5\right|$$

or

20, 3, 5

So the largest absolute value is in the Row 1. So as per Gaussian elimination with partial pivoting, the switch is between Row 1 and Row 1 to give

$$\begin{bmatrix} 20 & 15 & 10 \\ -3 & -2.249 & 7 \\ 5 & 1 & 3 \end{bmatrix} \begin{bmatrix} x_1 \\ x_2 \\ x_3 \end{bmatrix} = \begin{bmatrix} 45 \\ 1.751 \\ 9 \end{bmatrix}$$

Divide Row 1 by 20 and then multiply it by –3, that is, multiply Row 1 by $-3/20 = -0.15$.

$$([20 \quad 15 \quad 10] \quad [45]) \times -0.15 \text{ gives Row 1 as}$$

$$[-3 \quad -2.25 \quad -1.5] \quad [-6.75]$$

Subtract the result from Row 2

$$\begin{array}{r} [-3 \quad -2.249 \quad 7] \quad [1.751] \\ - [-3 \quad -2.25 \quad -1.5] \quad [-6.75] \\ \hline 0 \quad 0.001 \quad 8.5 \quad 8.501 \end{array}$$

to get the resulting equations as

$$\begin{bmatrix} 20 & 15 & 10 \\ 0 & 0.001 & 8.5 \\ 5 & 1 & 3 \end{bmatrix} \begin{bmatrix} x_1 \\ x_2 \\ x_3 \end{bmatrix} = \begin{bmatrix} 45 \\ 8.501 \\ 9 \end{bmatrix}$$

Divide Row 1 by 20 and then multiply it by 5, that is, multiply Row 1 by $5/20 = 0.25$.

$$([20 \quad 15 \quad 10] \quad [45]) \times 0.25 \text{ gives Row 1 as}$$

$$[5 \quad 3.75 \quad 2.5] \quad [11.25]$$

Subtract the result from Row 3

$$\begin{array}{r} [5 \quad 1 \quad 3] \quad [9] \\ - [5 \quad 3.75 \quad 2.5] \quad [11.25] \\ \hline 0 \quad -2.75 \quad 0.5 \quad -2.25 \end{array}$$

to get the resulting equations as

$$\begin{bmatrix} 20 & 15 & 10 \\ 0 & 0.001 & 8.5 \\ 0 & -2.75 & 0.5 \end{bmatrix} \begin{bmatrix} x_1 \\ x_2 \\ x_3 \end{bmatrix} = \begin{bmatrix} 45 \\ 8.501 \\ -2.25 \end{bmatrix}$$

This is the end of the first step of forward elimination.
Now for the second step of forward elimination, the absolute value of the second column elements below Row 1 is

$$\left|0.001\right|, \left|-2.75\right|$$

or

0.001, 2.75

So the largest absolute value is in Row 3. So Row 2 is switched with Row 3 to give

$$\begin{bmatrix} 20 & 15 & 10 \\ 0 & -2.75 & 0.5 \\ 0 & 0.001 & 8.5 \end{bmatrix} \begin{bmatrix} x_1 \\ x_2 \\ x_3 \end{bmatrix} = \begin{bmatrix} 7 \\ -2.25 \\ 8.501 \end{bmatrix}.$$

Divide Row 2 by -2.75 and then multiply it by 0.001, that is, multiply Row 2 by $0.001/-2.75 = -0.00036363$.

$$([0 \quad -2.75 \quad 0.5] \quad [-2.25]) \times -0.00036363 \text{ gives Row 2 as}$$

$$[0 \quad 0.00099998 \quad -0.00018182] \quad [0.00081816]$$

Subtract the result from Row 3

$$\begin{array}{r} [0 \quad\quad 0.001 \quad\quad\quad 8.5] \quad\quad\quad\quad [8.501] \\ - [0 \quad\quad 0.00099998 \quad -0.00018182] \quad [0.00081816] \\ \hline 0 \quad\quad 0 \quad\quad\quad\quad 8.50018182 \quad\quad 8.50018184 \end{array}$$

Rewriting within 5 significant digits with chopping

$$[0 \quad 0 \quad 8.5001] \quad [8.5001]$$

to get the resulting equations as

$$\begin{bmatrix} 20 & 15 & 10 \\ 0 & -2.75 & 0.5 \\ 0 & 0 & 8.5001 \end{bmatrix} \begin{bmatrix} x_1 \\ x_2 \\ x_3 \end{bmatrix} = \begin{bmatrix} 45 \\ -2.25 \\ 8.5001 \end{bmatrix}$$

Back substitution

$$8.5001x_3 = 8.5001$$

$$x_3 = \frac{8.5001}{8.5001}$$

$$= 1$$

Substituting the value of x_3 in Row 2

$$-2.75x_2 + 0.5x_3 = -2.25$$

$$x_2 = \frac{-2.25 - 0.5x_2}{-2.75}$$

$$= \frac{-2.25 - 0.5 \times 1}{-2.75}$$

$$= \frac{-2.25 - 0.5}{-2.75}$$

$$= \frac{-2.75}{-2.75}$$

$$= 1$$

Substituting the value of x_3 and x_2 in Row 1

$$20x_1 + 15x_2 + 10x_3 = 45$$

$$x_1 = \frac{45 - 15x_2 - 10x_3}{20}$$

$$= \frac{45 - 15 \times 1 - 10 \times 1}{20}$$

$$= \frac{45 - 15 - 10}{20}$$

$$= \frac{30 - 10}{20}$$

$$= \frac{20}{20}$$

$$= 1$$

So the solution is

$$[X] = \begin{bmatrix} x_1 \\ x_2 \\ x_3 \end{bmatrix}$$

$$= \begin{bmatrix} 1 \\ 1 \\ 1 \end{bmatrix}$$

This, in fact, is the exact solution. By coincidence only, in this case, the round-off error is fully removed.

Can we use Naïve Gauss elimination methods to find the determinant of a square matrix?

One of the more efficient ways to find the determinant of a square matrix is by taking advantage of the following two theorems on a determinant of matrices coupled with Naïve Gauss elimination.

Theorem 1:

Let $[A]$ be a $n \times n$ matrix. Then, if $[B]$ is a $n \times n$ matrix that results from adding or subtracting a multiple of one row to another row, then $\det(A) = \det(B)$ (The same is true for column operations also).

Theorem 2:

Let $[A]$ be a $n \times n$ matrix that is upper triangular, lower triangular or diagonal, then

$$\det(A) = a_{11} \times a_{22} \times ... \times a_{ii} \times ... \times a_{nn}$$

$$= \prod_{i=1}^{n} a_{ii}$$

This implies that if we apply the forward elimination steps of the Naïve Gauss elimination method, the determinant of the matrix stays the same according to Theorem 1. Then since at the end of the forward elimination steps, the resulting matrix is upper triangular, the determinant will be given by Theorem 2.

Example 5

Find the determinant of

$$[A] = \begin{bmatrix} 25 & 5 & 1 \\ 64 & 8 & 1 \\ 144 & 12 & 1 \end{bmatrix}$$

Solution

Remember in Example 1, we conducted the steps of forward elimination of unknowns using the Naïve Gauss elimination method on $[A]$ to give

$$[B] = \begin{bmatrix} 25 & 5 & 1 \\ 0 & -4.8 & -1.56 \\ 0 & 0 & 0.7 \end{bmatrix}$$

According to Theorem 2

$$\begin{aligned} \det(A) &= \det(B) \\ &= 25 \times (-4.8) \times 0.7 \\ &= -84.00 \end{aligned}$$

What if I cannot find the determinant of the matrix using the Naïve Gauss elimination method, for example, if I get division by zero problems during the Naïve Gauss elimination method?

Well, you can apply Gaussian elimination with partial pivoting. However, the determinant of the resulting upper triangular matrix may differ by a sign. The following theorem applies in addition to the previous two to find the determinant of a square matrix.

Theorem 3:

Let $[A]$ be a $n \times n$ matrix. Then, if $[B]$ is a matrix that results from switching one row with another row, then $\det(B) = -\det(A)$.

Example 6

Find the determinant of

$$[A] = \begin{bmatrix} 10 & -7 & 0 \\ -3 & 2.099 & 6 \\ 5 & -1 & 5 \end{bmatrix}$$

Solution

The end of the forward elimination steps of Gaussian elimination with partial pivoting, we would obtain

$$[B] = \begin{bmatrix} 10 & -7 & 0 \\ 0 & 2.5 & 5 \\ 0 & 0 & 6.002 \end{bmatrix}$$

$$\det(B) = 10 \times 2.5 \times 6.002$$

$$= 150.05$$

Since rows were switched once during the forward elimination steps of Gaussian elimination with partial pivoting,

$$\det(A) = -\det(B)$$
$$= -150.05$$

Example 7

Prove

$$\det(A) = \frac{1}{\det\left(A^{-1}\right)}$$

Solution

$$[A][A]^{-1} = [I]$$
$$\det\left(A\,A^{-1}\right) = \det(I)$$
$$\det(A)\det\left(A^{-1}\right) = 1$$
$$\det(A) = \frac{1}{\det\left(A^{-1}\right)}$$

If $[A]$ is a $n \times n$ matrix and $\det(A) \neq 0$, what other statements are equivalent to it?

1. $[A]$ is invertible.
2. $[A]^{-1}$ exists.
3. $[A][X] = [C]$ has a unique solution.
4. $[A][X] = [0]$ solution is $[X] = [\bar{0}]$.
5. $[A][A]^{-1} = [I] = [A]^{-1}[A]$.

Key Terms:

Naïve Gauss Elimination
Partial Pivoting
Determinant

Problem Set

Chapter 04.06
Gaussian Elimination

1. The goal of Forward Elimination steps in Naïve Gauss Elimination method is to reduce the coefficient matrix
   - (A) to a diagonal matrix
   - (B) to an upper triangular matrix
   - (C) to a lower triangular matrix
   - (D) to an identity matrix

2. Using a computer with four significant digits with chopping, use Naïve Gauss Elimination to solve
$$0.0030x_1 + 55.23x_2 = 58.12$$
$$6.239x_1 - 7.123x_2 = 47.23$$

3. Using a computer with four significant digits with chopping, use Gaussian Elimination with Partial Pivoting to solve
$$0.0030x_1 + 55.23x_2 = 58.12$$
$$6.239x_1 - 7.123x_2 = 47.23$$

4.
   - (A) Using a computer with four significant digits with chopping, use Naïve Gauss Elimination to solve
$$4x_1 + x_2 - x_3 = -2$$
$$5x_1 + x_2 + 2x_3 = 4$$
$$6x_1 + x_2 + x_3 = 6$$
   - (B) Using a computer with four significant digits with chopping, use Gaussian Elimination with Partial Pivoting to solve
$$4x_1 + x_2 - x_3 = -2$$
$$5x_1 + x_2 + 2x_3 = 4$$
$$6x_1 + x_2 + x_3 = 6$$

5. For
$$[A] = \begin{bmatrix} 10 & -7 & 0 \\ -3 & 2.099 & 6 \\ 5 & -1 & 5 \end{bmatrix}$$
Find the determinant of $[A]$ using Forward Elimination step of Naïve Gauss Elimination method.

6. One of the drawbacks of Naive-Gauss Elimination method is _____.

7. Division by zero during Forward Elimination steps in Gaussian elimination with Partial Pivoting method implies the coefficient matrix $[A]$ is _____.

8. One of the advantages of Gaussian Elimination with Partial Pivoting over Naive Gauss Elimination method is _____.

9. Show and explain clearly the first step of forward elimination of Naïve Gauss Elimination method for

$$\begin{bmatrix} 1 & 2 & 3 \\ 4 & 6 & 7 \\ 6 & 10 & 13 \end{bmatrix} \begin{bmatrix} a \\ b \\ c \end{bmatrix} = \begin{bmatrix} 6 \\ 18 \\ 30 \end{bmatrix}$$

10. Show and explain clearly the first step of Forward Elimination of Gaussian Elimination method with Partial Pivoting for

$$\begin{bmatrix} 1 & 2 & 3 \\ 4 & 6 & 7 \\ 6 & 10 & 13 \end{bmatrix} \begin{bmatrix} a \\ b \\ c \end{bmatrix} = \begin{bmatrix} 6 \\ 18 \\ 30 \end{bmatrix}$$

11. At the end of Forward Elimination steps using Naïve Gauss Elimination method on the coefficient matrix

$$[A] = \begin{bmatrix} 25 & c & 1 \\ 64 & a & 1 \\ 144 & b & 1 \end{bmatrix},$$

$[A]$ reduces to

$$[B] = \begin{bmatrix} 25 & 5 & 1 \\ 0 & -4.8 & -1.56 \\ 0 & 0 & 0.7 \end{bmatrix}.$$

What is the determinant of $[A]$?

12. At the end of Gauss Elimination steps on a set of three equations, I obtain the following system of equations. Now using a computer that uses only three signif digits with chopping, what is the value of unknowns using back substitution? S all your intermediate work.

$$\begin{bmatrix} 10 & -7 & 0 \\ 0 & 2.567 & 5 \\ 0 & 0 & 6.022 \end{bmatrix} \begin{bmatrix} x_1 \\ x_2 \\ x_3 \end{bmatrix} = \begin{bmatrix} 7 \\ 2.5 \\ 6.012 \end{bmatrix}$$

Answers to Selected Problems:

1. B

2. $x_1 = 26.66, x_2 = 1.051$

3. $x_1 = 8.769, x_2 = 1.051$

4. a) $(3,-13,1)$
   b) $(2.995,-12.98,1.001)$

5. -150.05

6. Division by zero

7. It implies that the co-efficient matrix is singular, that is, its determinant is zero and it is not invertible.

8. It overcomes the problem of division by zero

9. Dividing Row 1 by 1; multiplying it by 4 and subtracting the result from Row 2

$$\begin{bmatrix} 1 & 2 & 3 \\ 0 & -2 & -5 \\ 6 & 10 & 13 \end{bmatrix} \begin{bmatrix} a \\ b \\ c \end{bmatrix} = \begin{bmatrix} 6 \\ -6 \\ 30 \end{bmatrix}$$

Dividing Row 1 by 1; multiplying it by 6 and subtracting the result from Row 3

$$\begin{bmatrix} 1 & 2 & 3 \\ & 2 & -5 \\ & & \end{bmatrix} \begin{bmatrix} a \\ b \\ \end{bmatrix} = \begin{bmatrix} 6 \\ -6 \\ -6 \end{bmatrix}$$

switch Row 3 and Row 1.

and subtracting the result from Row 2

$$= \begin{bmatrix} 30 \\ -2 \\ 6 \end{bmatrix}$$

id subtracting the result from Row 3

$$\begin{bmatrix} 6 & 10 & 13 \\ 0 & -0.6667 & -1.667 \\ 0 & 0.3333 & 0.8333 \end{bmatrix} \begin{bmatrix} a \\ b \\ c \end{bmatrix} = \begin{bmatrix} 30 \\ -2 \\ 1 \end{bmatrix}$$

11. $\det(A) = \det(B)$
$$= 25 \times (-4.8) \times 0.7$$
$$= -84$$

12. $6.022x_3 = 6.012$
$$x_3 = \frac{6.012}{6.022}$$
$$= 0.998$$
$2.567x_2 + 5x_3 = 2.5$
$$x_2 = \frac{2.5 - 5(0.998)}{2.567} = -0.972$$
$10x_1 + (-7)x_2 = 7$
$$x_1 = \frac{7 + 7(-0.972)}{10} = 0.020$$

Chapter 04.07
LU Decomposition

After reading this chapter, you should be able to:

1. *identify when LU decomposition is numerically more efficient than Gaussian elimination,*
2. *decompose a nonsingular matrix into LU, and*
3. *show how LU decomposition is used to find the inverse of a matrix.*

I hear about LU decomposition used as a method to solve a set of simultaneous linear equations. What is it?

We already studied two numerical methods of finding the solution to simultaneous linear equations – Naïve Gauss elimination and Gaussian elimination with partial pivoting. Then, why do we need to learn another method? To appreciate why LU decomposition could be a better choice than the Gauss elimination techniques in some cases, let us discuss first what LU decomposition is about.

For a nonsingular matrix $[A]$ on which one can successfully conduct the Naïve Gauss elimination forward elimination steps, one can always write it as

$$[A] = [L][U]$$

where

$[L]$ = Lower triangular matrix

$[U]$ = Upper triangular matrix

Then if one is solving a set of equations

$$[A][X] = [C],$$

then

$$[L][U][X] = [C] \text{ as } ([A] = [L][U])$$

Multiplying both sides by $[L]^{-1}$,

$$[L]^{-1}[L][U][X] = [L]^{-1}[C]$$

04.07.1

$$[I][U][X] = [L]^{-1}[C] \text{ as } \left([L]^{-1}[L] = [I]\right)$$

$$[U][X] = [L]^{-1}[C] \text{ as } \left([I][U] = [U]\right)$$

Let

$$[L]^{-1}[C] = [Z]$$

then

$$[L][Z] = [C] \tag{1}$$

and

$$[U][X] = [Z] \tag{2}$$

So we can solve Equation (1) first for $[Z]$ by using forward substitution and then use Equation (2) to calculate the solution vector $[X]$ by back substitution.

This is all exciting but LU decomposition looks more complicated than Gaussian elimination. Do we use LU decomposition because it is computationally more efficient than Gaussian elimination to solve a set of n equations given by $[A][X]=[C]$?

For a square matrix $[A]$ of $n \times n$ size, the computational time[1] $CT\,|_{DE}$ to decompose the $[A]$ matrix to $[L][U]$ form is given by

$$CT\,|_{DE} = T\left(\frac{8n^3}{3} + 4n^2 - \frac{20n}{3}\right),$$

where

T = clock cycle time[2].

The computational time $CT\,|_{FS}$ to solve by forward substitution $[L][Z]=[C]$ is given by

$$CT\,|_{FS} = T\left(4n^2 - 4n\right)$$

The computational time $CT\,|_{BS}$ to solve by back substitution $[U][X]=[Z]$ is given by

$$CT\,|_{BS} = T\left(4n^2 + 12n\right)$$

So, the total computational time to solve a set of equations by LU decomposition is

$$CT\,|_{LU} = CT\,|_{DE} + CT\,|_{FS} + CT\,|_{BS}$$

$$= T\left(\frac{8n^3}{3} + 4n^2 - \frac{20n}{3}\right) + T\left(4n^2 - 4n\right) + T\left(4n^2 + 12n\right)$$

$$= T\left(\frac{8n^3}{3} + 12n^2 + \frac{4n}{3}\right)$$

---

[1] The time is calculated by first separately calculating the number of additions, subtractions, multiplications, and divisions in a procedure such as back substitution, etc. We then assume 4 clock cycles each for an add, subtract, or multiply operation, and 16 clock cycles for a divide operation as is the case for a typical AMD®-K7 chip.
http://www.isi.edu/~draper/papers/mwscas07_kwon.pdf

[2] As an example, a 1.2 GHz CPU has a clock cycle of $1/(1.2 \times 10^9) = 0.833333\,\text{ns}$

Now let us look at the computational time taken by Gaussian elimination. The computational time $CT|_{FE}$ for the forward elimination part,

$$CT|_{FE} = T\left(\frac{8n^3}{3} + 8n^2 - \frac{32n}{3}\right),$$

and the computational time $CT|_{BS}$ for the back substitution part is

$$CT|_{BS} = T\left(4n^2 + 12n\right)$$

So, the total computational time $CT|_{GE}$ to solve a set of equations by Gaussian Elimination is

$$CT|_{GE} = CT|_{FE} + CT|_{BS}$$

$$= T\left(\frac{8n^3}{3} + 8n^2 - \frac{32n}{3}\right) + T\left(4n^2 + 12n\right)$$

$$= T\left(\frac{8n^3}{3} + 12n^2 + \frac{4n}{3}\right)$$

The computational time for Gaussian elimination and LU decomposition is identical.

This has confused me further! Why learn LU decomposition method when it takes the same computational time as Gaussian elimination, and that too when the two methods are closely related. Please convince me that LU decomposition has its place in solving linear equations!

We have the knowledge now to convince you that LU decomposition method has its place in the solution of simultaneous linear equations. Let us look at an example where the LU decomposition method is computationally more efficient than Gaussian elimination. Remember in trying to find the inverse of the matrix $[A]$ in Chapter 04.05, the problem reduces to solving n sets of equations with the n columns of the identity matrix as the RHS vector. For calculations of each column of the inverse of the $[A]$ matrix, the coefficient matrix $[A]$ matrix in the set of equation $[A][X] = [C]$ does not change. So if we use the LU decomposition method, the $[A] = [L][U]$ decomposition needs to be done only once, the forward substitution (Equation 1) n times, and the back substitution (Equation 2) n times.

So the total computational time $CT|_{inverse\,LU}$ required to find the inverse of a matrix using LU decomposition is

$$CT|_{inverse\,LU} = 1 \times CT|_{LU} + n \times CT|_{FS} + n \times CT|_{BS}$$

$$= 1 \times T\left(\frac{8n^3}{3} + 4n^2 - \frac{20n}{3}\right) + n \times T\left(4n^2 - 4n\right) + n \times T\left(4n^2 + 12n\right)$$

$$= T\left(\frac{32n^3}{3} + 12n^2 - \frac{20n}{3}\right)$$

In comparison, if Gaussian elimination method were used to find the inverse of a matrix, the forward elimination as well as the back substitution will have to be done n times. The total computational time $CT|_{inverse\,GE}$ required to find the inverse of a matrix by using Gaussian elimination then is

$$CT|_{inverse\,GE} = n \times CT|_{FE} + n \times CT|_{BS}$$

$$= n \times T\left(\frac{8n^3}{3} + 8n^2 - \frac{32n}{3}\right) + n \times T\left(4n^2 + 12n\right)$$

$$= T\left(\frac{8n^4}{3} + 12n^3 + \frac{4n^2}{3}\right)$$

Clearly for large n, $CT|_{inverse\,GE} >> CT|_{inverse\,LU}$ as $CT|_{inverse\,GE}$ has the dominating terms of n^4 and $CT|_{inverse\,LU}$ has the dominating terms of n^3. For large values of n, Gaussian elimination method would take more computational time (approximately $n/4$ times – prove it) than the LU decomposition method. Typical values of the ratio of the computational time for different values of n are given in Table 1.

Table 1 Comparing computational times of finding inverse of a matrix using LU decomposition and Gaussian elimination.

n	10	100	1000	10000
$CT|_{inverse\,GE}/CT|_{inverse\,LU}$	3.28	25.83	250.8	2501

Are you convinced now that LU decomposition has its place in solving systems of equations? We are now ready to answer other curious questions such as
1) How do I find LU matrices for a nonsingular matrix $[A]$?
2) How do I conduct forward and back substitution steps of Equations (1) and (2), respectively?

How do I decompose a non-singular matrix $[A]$, that is, how do I find $[A] = [L][U]$?

If forward elimination steps of the Naïve Gauss elimination methods can be applied on a nonsingular matrix, then $[A]$ can be decomposed into LU as

$$[A] = \begin{bmatrix} a_{11} & a_{12} & \cdots & a_{1n} \\ a_{21} & a_{22} & \cdots & a_{2n} \\ \vdots & \vdots & \cdots & \vdots \\ a_{n1} & a_{n2} & \cdots & a_{nn} \end{bmatrix}$$

$$= \begin{bmatrix} 1 & 0 & \cdots & 0 \\ \ell_{21} & 1 & \cdots & 0 \\ \vdots & \vdots & \cdots & \vdots \\ \ell_{n1} & \ell_{n2} & \cdots & 1 \end{bmatrix} \begin{bmatrix} u_{11} & u_{12} & \cdots & u_{1n} \\ 0 & u_{22} & \cdots & u_{2n} \\ \vdots & \vdots & \cdots & \vdots \\ 0 & 0 & \cdots & u_{nn} \end{bmatrix}$$

The elements of the $[U]$ matrix are exactly the same as the coefficient matrix one obtains at the end of the forward elimination steps in Naïve Gauss elimination.

The lower triangular matrix $[L]$ has 1 in its diagonal entries. The non-zero elements on the non-diagonal elements in $[L]$ are multipliers that made the corresponding entries zero in the upper triangular matrix $[U]$ during forward elimination.

Let us look at this using the same example as used in Naïve Gaussian elimination.

Example 1

Find the LU decomposition of the matrix

$$[A] = \begin{bmatrix} 25 & 5 & 1 \\ 64 & 8 & 1 \\ 144 & 12 & 1 \end{bmatrix}$$

Solution

$$[A] = [L][U]$$

$$= \begin{bmatrix} 1 & 0 & 0 \\ \ell_{21} & 1 & 0 \\ \ell_{31} & \ell_{32} & 1 \end{bmatrix} \begin{bmatrix} u_{11} & u_{12} & u_{13} \\ 0 & u_{22} & u_{23} \\ 0 & 0 & u_{33} \end{bmatrix}$$

The $[U]$ matrix is the same as found at the end of the forward elimination of Naïve Gauss elimination method, that is

$$[U] = \begin{bmatrix} 25 & 5 & 1 \\ 0 & -4.8 & -1.56 \\ 0 & 0 & 0.7 \end{bmatrix}$$

To find ℓ_{21} and ℓ_{31}, find the multiplier that was used to make the a_{21} and a_{31} elements zero in the first step of forward elimination of the Naïve Gauss elimination method. It was

$$\ell_{21} = \frac{64}{25}$$
$$= 2.56$$

$$\ell_{31} = \frac{144}{25}$$
$$= 5.76$$

To find ℓ_{32}, what multiplier was used to make a_{32} element zero? Remember a_{32} element was made zero in the second step of forward elimination. The $[A]$ matrix at the beginning of the second step of forward elimination was

$$\begin{bmatrix} 25 & 5 & 1 \\ 0 & -4.8 & -1.56 \\ 0 & -16.8 & -4.76 \end{bmatrix}$$

So

$$\ell_{32} = \frac{-16.8}{-4.8}$$
$$= 3.5$$

Hence

$$[L] = \begin{bmatrix} 1 & 0 & 0 \\ 2.56 & 1 & 0 \\ 5.76 & 3.5 & 1 \end{bmatrix}$$

Confirm $[L][U] = [A]$.

$$[L][U] = \begin{bmatrix} 1 & 0 & 0 \\ 2.56 & 1 & 0 \\ 5.76 & 3.5 & 1 \end{bmatrix} \begin{bmatrix} 25 & 5 & 1 \\ 0 & -4.8 & -1.56 \\ 0 & 0 & 0.7 \end{bmatrix}$$

$$= \begin{bmatrix} 25 & 5 & 1 \\ 64 & 8 & 1 \\ 144 & 12 & 1 \end{bmatrix}$$

Example 2

Use the LU decomposition method to solve the following simultaneous linear equations.

$$\begin{bmatrix} 25 & 5 & 1 \\ 64 & 8 & 1 \\ 144 & 12 & 1 \end{bmatrix} \begin{bmatrix} a_1 \\ a_2 \\ a_3 \end{bmatrix} = \begin{bmatrix} 106.8 \\ 177.2 \\ 279.2 \end{bmatrix}$$

Solution

Recall that
$$[A][X] = [C]$$
and if
$$[A] = [L][U]$$
then first solving
$$[L][Z] = [C]$$
and then
$$[U][X] = [Z]$$
gives the solution vector $[X]$.

Now in the previous example, we showed
$$[A] = [L][U]$$

$$= \begin{bmatrix} 1 & 0 & 0 \\ 2.56 & 1 & 0 \\ 5.76 & 3.5 & 1 \end{bmatrix} \begin{bmatrix} 25 & 5 & 1 \\ 0 & -4.8 & -1.56 \\ 0 & 0 & 0.7 \end{bmatrix}$$

First solve
$$[L][Z] = [C]$$

$$\begin{bmatrix} 1 & 0 & 0 \\ 2.56 & 1 & 0 \\ 5.76 & 3.5 & 1 \end{bmatrix} \begin{bmatrix} z_1 \\ z_2 \\ z_3 \end{bmatrix} = \begin{bmatrix} 106.8 \\ 177.2 \\ 279.2 \end{bmatrix}$$

to give

$$z_1 = 106.8$$
$$2.56z_1 + z_2 = 177.2$$
$$5.76z_1 + 3.5z_2 + z_3 = 279.2$$

Forward substitution starting from the first equation gives

$$z_1 = 106.8$$
$$z_2 = 177.2 - 2.56z_1$$
$$= 177.2 - 2.56 \times 106.8$$
$$= -96.208$$
$$z_3 = 279.2 - 5.76z_1 - 3.5z_2$$
$$= 279.2 - 5.76 \times 106.8 - 3.5 \times (-96.208)$$
$$= 0.76$$

Hence

$$[Z] = \begin{bmatrix} z_1 \\ z_2 \\ z_3 \end{bmatrix}$$

$$= \begin{bmatrix} 106.8 \\ -96.208 \\ 0.76 \end{bmatrix}$$

This matrix is same as the right hand side obtained at the end of the forward elimination steps of Naïve Gauss elimination method. Is this a coincidence?

Now solve

$$[U][X] = [Z]$$

$$\begin{bmatrix} 25 & 5 & 1 \\ 0 & -4.8 & -1.56 \\ 0 & 0 & 0.7 \end{bmatrix} \begin{bmatrix} a_1 \\ a_2 \\ a_3 \end{bmatrix} = \begin{bmatrix} 106.8 \\ -96.208 \\ 0.76 \end{bmatrix}$$

$$25a_1 + 5a_2 + a_3 = 106.8$$
$$-4.8a_2 - 1.56a_3 = -96.208$$
$$0.7a_3 = 0.76$$

From the third equation

$$0.7a_3 = 0.76$$
$$a_3 = \frac{0.76}{0.7}$$
$$= 1.0857$$

Substituting the value of a_3 in the second equation,

$$-4.8a_2 - 1.56a_3 = -96.208$$
$$a_2 = \frac{-96.208 + 1.56a_3}{-4.8}$$
$$= \frac{-96.208 + 1.56 \times 1.0857}{-4.8}$$

$$= 19.691$$

Substituting the value of a_2 and a_3 in the first equation,

$$25a_1 + 5a_2 + a_3 = 106.8$$

$$a_1 = \frac{106.8 - 5a_2 - a_3}{25}$$

$$= \frac{106.8 - 5 \times 19.691 - 1.0857}{25}$$

$$= 0.29048$$

Hence the solution vector is

$$\begin{bmatrix} a_1 \\ a_2 \\ a_3 \end{bmatrix} = \begin{bmatrix} 0.29048 \\ 19.691 \\ 1.0857 \end{bmatrix}$$

How do I find the inverse of a square matrix using LU decomposition?

A matrix $[B]$ is the inverse of $[A]$ if

$$[A][B] = [I] = [B][A].$$

How can we use LU decomposition to find the inverse of the matrix? Assume the first column of $[B]$ (the inverse of $[A]$) is

$$[b_{11} \, b_{12} \, \ldots \, \ldots \, b_{n1}]^{\mathrm{T}}$$

Then from the above definition of an inverse and the definition of matrix multiplication

$$[A] \begin{bmatrix} b_{11} \\ b_{21} \\ \vdots \\ b_{n1} \end{bmatrix} = \begin{bmatrix} 1 \\ 0 \\ \vdots \\ 0 \end{bmatrix}$$

Similarly the second column of $[B]$ is given by

$$[A] \begin{bmatrix} b_{12} \\ b_{22} \\ \vdots \\ b_{n2} \end{bmatrix} = \begin{bmatrix} 0 \\ 1 \\ \vdots \\ 0 \end{bmatrix}$$

Similarly, all columns of $[B]$ can be found by solving n different sets of equations with the column of the right hand side being the n columns of the identity matrix.

Example 3

Use LU decomposition to find the inverse of

$$[A] = \begin{bmatrix} 25 & 5 & 1 \\ 64 & 8 & 1 \\ 144 & 12 & 1 \end{bmatrix}$$

Solution

Knowing that

$$[A] = [L][U]$$

$$= \begin{bmatrix} 1 & 0 & 0 \\ 2.56 & 1 & 0 \\ 5.76 & 3.5 & 1 \end{bmatrix} \begin{bmatrix} 25 & 5 & 1 \\ 0 & -4.8 & -1.56 \\ 0 & 0 & 0.7 \end{bmatrix}$$

We can solve for the first column of $[B] = [A]^{-1}$ by solving for

$$\begin{bmatrix} 25 & 5 & 1 \\ 64 & 8 & 1 \\ 144 & 12 & 1 \end{bmatrix} \begin{bmatrix} b_{11} \\ b_{21} \\ b_{31} \end{bmatrix} = \begin{bmatrix} 1 \\ 0 \\ 0 \end{bmatrix}$$

First solve

$$[L][Z] = [C],$$

that is

$$\begin{bmatrix} 1 & 0 & 0 \\ 2.56 & 1 & 0 \\ 5.76 & 3.5 & 1 \end{bmatrix} \begin{bmatrix} z_1 \\ z_2 \\ z_3 \end{bmatrix} = \begin{bmatrix} 1 \\ 0 \\ 0 \end{bmatrix}$$

to give

$$z_1 = 1$$
$$2.56z_1 + z_2 = 0$$
$$5.76z_1 + 3.5z_2 + z_3 = 0$$

Forward substitution starting from the first equation gives

$$z_1 = 1$$
$$\begin{aligned} z_2 &= 0 - 2.56z_1 \\ &= 0 - 2.56(1) \\ &= -2.56 \end{aligned}$$
$$\begin{aligned} z_3 &= 0 - 5.76z_1 - 3.5z_2 \\ &= 0 - 5.76(1) - 3.5(-2.56) \\ &= 3.2 \end{aligned}$$

Hence

$$[Z] = \begin{bmatrix} z_1 \\ z_2 \\ z_3 \end{bmatrix}$$

$$= \begin{bmatrix} 1 \\ -2.56 \\ 3.2 \end{bmatrix}$$

Now solve

$$[U][X] = [Z]$$

that is

$$\begin{bmatrix} 25 & 5 & 1 \\ 0 & -4.8 & -1.56 \\ 0 & 0 & 0.7 \end{bmatrix} \begin{bmatrix} b_{11} \\ b_{21} \\ b_{31} \end{bmatrix} = \begin{bmatrix} 1 \\ -2.56 \\ 3.2 \end{bmatrix}$$

$$25b_{11} + 5b_{21} + b_{31} = 1$$
$$-4.8b_{21} - 1.56b_{31} = -2.56$$
$$0.7b_{31} = 3.2$$

Backward substitution starting from the third equation gives

$$b_{31} = \frac{3.2}{0.7}$$
$$= 4.571$$
$$b_{21} = \frac{-2.56 + 1.56b_{31}}{-4.8}$$
$$= \frac{-2.56 + 1.56(4.571)}{-4.8}$$
$$= -0.9524$$
$$b_{11} = \frac{1 - 5b_{21} - b_{31}}{25}$$
$$= \frac{1 - 5(-0.9524) - 4.571}{25}$$
$$= 0.04762$$

Hence the first column of the inverse of $[A]$ is

$$\begin{bmatrix} b_{11} \\ b_{21} \\ b_{31} \end{bmatrix} = \begin{bmatrix} 0.04762 \\ -0.9524 \\ 4.571 \end{bmatrix}$$

Similarly by solving

$$\begin{bmatrix} 25 & 5 & 1 \\ 64 & 8 & 1 \\ 144 & 12 & 1 \end{bmatrix} \begin{bmatrix} b_{12} \\ b_{22} \\ b_{32} \end{bmatrix} = \begin{bmatrix} 0 \\ 1 \\ 0 \end{bmatrix} \text{ gives } \begin{bmatrix} b_{12} \\ b_{22} \\ b_{32} \end{bmatrix} = \begin{bmatrix} -0.08333 \\ 1.417 \\ -5.000 \end{bmatrix}$$

and solving

$$\begin{bmatrix} 25 & 5 & 1 \\ 64 & 8 & 1 \\ 144 & 12 & 1 \end{bmatrix} \begin{bmatrix} b_{13} \\ b_{23} \\ b_{33} \end{bmatrix} = \begin{bmatrix} 0 \\ 0 \\ 1 \end{bmatrix} \text{ gives } \begin{bmatrix} b_{13} \\ b_{23} \\ b_{33} \end{bmatrix} = \begin{bmatrix} 0.03571 \\ -0.4643 \\ 1.429 \end{bmatrix}$$

Hence

$$[A]^{-1} = \begin{bmatrix} 0.04762 & -0.08333 & 0.03571 \\ -0.9524 & 1.417 & -0.4643 \\ 4.571 & -5.000 & 1.429 \end{bmatrix}$$

Can you confirm the following for the above example?

$$[A][A]^{-1} = [I] = [A]^{-1}[A]$$

Key Terms:

LU decomposition
Inverse

Problem Set

Chapter 04.07
LU Decomposition

1. Show that LU decomposition is computationally more efficient way of finding the inverse of a square matrix than using Gaussian elimination.

2. LU decomposition method is computationally more efficient than Naïve Gauss elimination for
   (A) Solving a single set of simultaneous linear equations
   (B) Solving multiple sets of simultaneous linear equations with different coefficient matrices.
   (C) Solving multiple sets of simultaneous linear equations with same coefficient matrix but different right hand sides.
   (D) Solving less than ten simultaneous linear equations.

3. If one decomposes a symmetric matrix $[A]$ to a LU form, then
   (A) $[L] = [U]^T$
   (B) $[U]^T = [L]^T$
   (C) $[L] = [U]$
   (D) $[L] = [I]$

4. Use LU decomposition to solve
   $$4x_1 + x_2 - x_3 = -2$$
   $$5x_1 + x_2 + 2x_3 = 4$$
   $$6x_1 + x_2 + x_3 = 6$$

5. Find the inverse of
   $$[A] = \begin{bmatrix} 3 & 4 & 1 \\ 2 & -7 & -1 \\ 8 & 1 & 5 \end{bmatrix}$$
   using LU decomposition

6. Show that the nonsingular matrix
   $$[A] = \begin{bmatrix} 0 & 2 \\ 2 & 0 \end{bmatrix}$$
   cannot be decomposed into LU form.

7. For large values of n for a $n \times n$ matrix $[A]$, the computational time taken to find the inverse of $[A]$ by using Naïve Gaussian Elimination Method is proportional to $n^4/3 + n^3/2$ and by using $[L][U]$ decomposition method is proportional to $4n^3/3$. If it takes 15 seconds to find the inverse of a 2500×2500 matrix by using $[L][U]$ decomposition method, estimate the time it would take to find the inverse of a 2500×2500 matrix by using Naive Gaussian Elimination Method.

Answers to Selected Problems:

1. For large values of size of matrix, n, Gaussian elimination takes $\frac{n}{4}$ times the time that LU decomposition would for finding the inverse of a matrix.

2. C

3. A

4. $(3,-13,1)$

5. $$[A]^{-1} = \begin{bmatrix} 2.931 \times 10^{-1} & 1.638 \times 10^{-1} & -2.586 \times 10^{-2} \\ 1.552 \times 10^{-1} & -6.034 \times 10^{-2} & -4.310 \times 10^{-2} \\ -5.000 \times 10^{-1} & -2.500 \times 10^{-1} & 2.500 \times 10^{-1} \end{bmatrix}$$

6. Try to find the unknowns in
$$\begin{bmatrix} 1 & 0 \\ \ell_{21} & 1 \end{bmatrix} \begin{bmatrix} u_{11} & u_{12} \\ 0 & u_{22} \end{bmatrix} = \begin{bmatrix} 0 & 2 \\ 2 & 0 \end{bmatrix}$$
Do you see any inconsistencies? Understand that
$$\begin{bmatrix} 0 & 2 \\ 2 & 0 \end{bmatrix}$$
is nonsingular.

7. 9375 seconds.

Chapter 04.08
Gauss-Seidel Method

After reading this chapter, you should be able to:
1. *solve a set of equations using the Gauss-Seidel method,*
2. *recognize the advantages and pitfalls of the Gauss-Seidel method, and*
3. *determine under what conditions the Gauss-Seidel method always converges.*

Why do we need another method to solve a set of simultaneous linear equations?

In certain cases, such as when a system of equations is large, iterative methods of solving equations are more advantageous. Elimination methods, such as Gaussian elimination, are prone to large round-off errors for a large set of equations. Iterative methods, such as the Gauss-Seidel method, give the user control of the round-off error. Also, if the physics of the problem are well known, initial guesses needed in iterative methods can be made more judiciously leading to faster convergence.

What is the algorithm for the Gauss-Seidel method? Given a general set of n equations and n unknowns, we have

$$a_{11}x_1 + a_{12}x_2 + a_{13}x_3 + ... + a_{1n}x_n = c_1$$
$$a_{21}x_1 + a_{22}x_2 + a_{23}x_3 + ... + a_{2n}x_n = c_2$$

$$\begin{matrix} . & & . \\ . & & . \\ . & & . \end{matrix}$$

$$a_{n1}x_1 + a_{n2}x_2 + a_{n3}x_3 + ... + a_{nn}x_n = c_n$$

If the diagonal elements are non-zero, each equation is rewritten for the corresponding unknown, that is, the first equation is rewritten with x_1 on the left hand side, the second equation is rewritten with x_2 on the left hand side and so on as follows

$$x_2 = \frac{c_2 - a_{21}x_1 - a_{23}x_3 \dots - a_{2n}x_n}{a_{22}}$$

$$\vdots$$
$$\vdots$$

$$x_{n-1} = \frac{c_{n-1} - a_{n-1,1}x_1 - a_{n-1,2}x_2 \dots - a_{n-1,n-2}x_{n-2} - a_{n-1,n}x_n}{a_{n-1,n-1}}$$

$$x_n = \frac{c_n - a_{n1}x_1 - a_{n2}x_2 - \dots - a_{n,n-1}x_{n-1}}{a_{nn}}$$

These equations can be rewritten in a summation form as

$$x_1 = \frac{c_1 - \sum_{\substack{j=1 \\ j \neq 1}}^{n} a_{1j}x_j}{a_{11}}$$

$$x_2 = \frac{c_2 - \sum_{\substack{j=1 \\ j \neq 2}}^{n} a_{2j}x_j}{a_{22}}$$

$$\cdot$$
$$\cdot$$
$$\cdot$$

$$x_{n-1} = \frac{c_{n-1} - \sum_{\substack{j=1 \\ j \neq n-1}}^{n} a_{n-1,j}x_j}{a_{n-1,n-1}}$$

$$x_n = \frac{c_n - \sum_{\substack{j=1 \\ j \neq n}}^{n} a_{nj}x_j}{a_{nn}}$$

Hence for any row i,

$$x_i = \frac{c_i - \sum_{\substack{j=1 \\ j \neq i}}^{n} a_{ij}x_j}{a_{ii}}, i = 1,2,\dots,n.$$

Now to find x_i's, one assumes an initial guess for the x_i's and then uses the rewritten equations to calculate the new estimates. Remember, one always uses the most recent estimates to calculate the next estimates, x_i. At the end of each iteration, one calculates the absolute relative approximate error for each x_i as

$$\left|\in_a\right|_i = \left|\frac{x_i^{new} - x_i^{old}}{x_i^{new}}\right| \times 100$$

where x_i^{new} is the recently obtained value of x_i, and x_i^{old} is the previous value of x_i.

When the absolute relative approximate error for each x_i is less than the pre-specified tolerance, the iterations are stopped.

Example 1

The upward velocity of a rocket is given at three different times in the following table

Table 1 Velocity vs. time data.

Time, t (s)	Velocity, v (m/s)
5	106.8
8	177.2
12	279.2

The velocity data is approximated by a polynomial as
$$v(t) = a_1 t^2 + a_2 t + a_3 , \qquad 5 \le t \le 12$$
Find the values of a_1, a_2, and a_3 using the Gauss-Seidel method. Assume an initial guess of the solution as
$$\begin{bmatrix} a_1 \\ a_2 \\ a_3 \end{bmatrix} = \begin{bmatrix} 1 \\ 2 \\ 5 \end{bmatrix}$$
and conduct two iterations.

Solution

The polynomial is going through three data points $(t_1, v_1), (t_2, v_2)$, and (t_3, v_3) where from the above table
$$t_1 = 5, \quad v_1 = 106.8$$
$$t_2 = 8, \quad v_2 = 177.2$$
$$t_3 = 12, \quad v_3 = 279.2$$
Requiring that $v(t) = a_1 t^2 + a_2 t + a_3$ passes through the three data points gives
$$v(t_1) = v_1 = a_1 t_1^2 + a_2 t_1 + a_3$$
$$v(t_2) = v_2 = a_1 t_2^2 + a_2 t_2 + a_3$$
$$v(t_3) = v_3 = a_1 t_3^2 + a_2 t_3 + a_3$$
Substituting the data $(t_1, v_1), (t_2, v_2)$, and (t_3, v_3) gives
$$a_1(5^2) + a_2(5) + a_3 = 106.8$$
$$a_1(8^2) + a_2(8) + a_3 = 177.2$$
$$a_1(12^2) + a_2(12) + a_3 = 279.2$$
or
$$25a_1 + 5a_2 + a_3 = 106.8$$
$$64a_1 + 8a_2 + a_3 = 177.2$$

$$144a_1 + 12a_2 + a_3 = 279.2$$

The coefficients $a_1, a_2,$ and a_3 for the above expression are given by

$$\begin{bmatrix} 25 & 5 & 1 \\ 64 & 8 & 1 \\ 144 & 12 & 1 \end{bmatrix} \begin{bmatrix} a_1 \\ a_2 \\ a_3 \end{bmatrix} = \begin{bmatrix} 106.8 \\ 177.2 \\ 279.2 \end{bmatrix}$$

Rewriting the equations gives

$$a_1 = \frac{106.8 - 5a_2 - a_3}{25}$$

$$a_2 = \frac{177.2 - 64a_1 - a_3}{8}$$

$$a_3 = \frac{279.2 - 144a_1 - 12a_2}{1}$$

Iteration #1

Given the initial guess of the solution vector as

$$\begin{bmatrix} a_1 \\ a_2 \\ a_3 \end{bmatrix} = \begin{bmatrix} 1 \\ 2 \\ 5 \end{bmatrix}$$

we get

$$a_1 = \frac{106.8 - 5(2) - (5)}{25}$$

$$= 3.6720$$

$$a_2 = \frac{177.2 - 64(3.6720)}{8}$$

$$= -7.8150$$

$$a_3 = \frac{279.2 - 144(3.6\ }{ }$$

$$= -155.36$$

The absolute relative apr

$$|\epsilon_a|_1 = \left| \frac{3.6720 - }{3.672} \right.$$

$$= 72.76$$

$$|\epsilon_a|_2 = \left| \frac{-7.}{ } \right.$$

$$= 1$$

$$|\epsilon_a|_3 = \left| \frac{ }{ } \right.$$

$$= 1($$

At the end of the

At the end of the second iterat

$$= 80.540\%$$

$$|\epsilon_a|_3 = \left| \frac{12.056}{-54.882} \right.$$

$$|\epsilon_a|_2 = \left| \frac{-798.}{ } \right.$$

$$= 85.6$$

$$\begin{bmatrix} \ \\ -54.882 \end{bmatrix}$$

$$-798.54$$

absolute relative approx
iterations gives the foll
te relative approximate er

$$\begin{bmatrix} a_1 \\ a_2 \\ a_3 \end{bmatrix} = \begin{bmatrix} 3.6720 \\ -7.8510 \\ -155.36 \end{bmatrix}$$

and the maximum absolute relative approximate error is 125.47%.

Iteration #2
The estimate of the solution vector at the end of Iteration #1 is

$$\begin{bmatrix} a_1 \\ a_2 \\ a_3 \end{bmatrix} = \begin{bmatrix} 3.6720 \\ -7.8510 \\ -155.36 \end{bmatrix}$$

Now we get

$$a_1 = \frac{106.8 - 5(-7.8510) - (-155.36)}{25}$$

$$= 12.056$$

$$a_2 = \frac{177.2 - 64(12.056) - (-155.36)}{8}$$

$$= -54.882$$

$$a_3 = \frac{279.2 - 144(12.056) - 12(-54.882)}{1}$$

$$= -798.34$$

The absolute relative approximate error for each x_i then is

$$|\epsilon_a|_1 = \left| \frac{12.056 - 3.6720}{12.056} \right| \times 100$$

$$= 69.543\%$$

$$\left| \frac{-54.882 - (-7.8510)}{-54.882} \right| \times 100$$

$$\;5\%$$

$$\left| \frac{\;4 - (-155.36)}{\;8.34} \right| \times 100$$

on the estimate of the solution vector is

imate error is 85.695%.
wing values for the solution vector and the
ors.

Iteration	a_1	$\left|\epsilon_a\right|_1\%$	a_2	$\left|\epsilon_a\right|_2\%$	a_3	$\left|\epsilon_a\right|_3\%$
1	3.6720	72.767	−7.8510	125.47	−155.36	103.22
2	12.056	69.543	−54.882	85.695	−798.34	80.540
3	47.182	74.447	−255.51	78.521	−3448.9	76.852
4	193.33	75.595	−1093.4	76.632	−14440	76.116
5	800.53	75.850	−4577.2	76.112	−60072	75.963
6	3322.6	75.906	−19049	75.972	−249580	75.931

As seen in the above table, the solution estimates are not converging to the true solution of
$$a_1 = 0.29048$$
$$a_2 = 19.690$$
$$a_3 = 1.0857$$

The above system of equations does not seem to converge. Why?

Well, a pitfall of most iterative methods is that they may or may not converge. However, the solution to a certain classes of systems of simultaneous equations does always converge using the Gauss-Seidel method. This class of system of equations is where the coefficient matrix $[A]$ in $[A][X] = [C]$ is diagonally dominant, that is

$$\left|a_{ii}\right| \geq \sum_{\substack{j=1 \\ j \neq i}}^{n} \left|a_{ij}\right| \text{ for all } i$$

$$\left|a_{ii}\right| > \sum_{\substack{j=1 \\ j \neq i}}^{n} \left|a_{ij}\right| \text{ for at least one } i$$

If a system of equations has a coefficient matrix that is not diagonally dominant, it may or may not converge. Fortunately, many physical systems that result in simultaneous linear equations have a diagonally dominant coefficient matrix, which then assures convergence for iterative methods such as the Gauss-Seidel method of solving simultaneous linear equations.

Example 2

Find the solution to the following system of equations using the Gauss-Seidel method.
$$12x_1 + 3x_2 - 5x_3 = 1$$
$$x_1 + 5x_2 + 3x_3 = 28$$
$$3x_1 + 7x_2 + 13x_3 = 76$$

Use
$$\begin{bmatrix} x_1 \\ x_2 \\ x_3 \end{bmatrix} = \begin{bmatrix} 1 \\ 0 \\ 1 \end{bmatrix}$$

as the initial guess and conduct two iterations.
Solution

The coefficient matrix

$$[A] = \begin{bmatrix} 12 & 3 & -5 \\ 1 & 5 & 3 \\ 3 & 7 & 13 \end{bmatrix}$$

is diagonally dominant as

$$|a_{11}| = |12| = 12 \geq |a_{12}| + |a_{13}| = |3| + |-5| = 8$$
$$|a_{22}| = |5| = 5 \geq |a_{21}| + |a_{23}| = |1| + |3| = 4$$
$$|a_{33}| = |13| = 13 \geq |a_{31}| + |a_{32}| = |3| + |7| = 10$$

and the inequality is strictly greater than for at least one row. Hence, the solution should converge using the Gauss-Seidel method.

Rewriting the equations, we get

$$x_1 = \frac{1 - 3x_2 + 5x_3}{12}$$

$$x_2 = \frac{28 - x_1 - 3x_3}{5}$$

$$x_3 = \frac{76 - 3x_1 - 7x_2}{13}$$

Assuming an initial guess of

$$\begin{bmatrix} x_1 \\ x_2 \\ x_3 \end{bmatrix} = \begin{bmatrix} 1 \\ 0 \\ 1 \end{bmatrix}$$

Iteration #1

$$x_1 = \frac{1 - 3(0) + 5(1)}{12}$$
$$= 0.50000$$

$$x_2 = \frac{28 - (0.50000) - 3(1)}{5}$$
$$= 4.9000$$

$$x_3 = \frac{76 - 3(0.50000) - 7(4.9000)}{13}$$
$$= 3.0923$$

The absolute relative approximate error at the end of the first iteration is

$$|\epsilon_a|_1 = \left| \frac{0.50000 - 1}{0.50000} \right| \times 100$$
$$= 100.00\%$$

$$|\epsilon_a|_2 = \left| \frac{4.9000 - 0}{4.9000} \right| \times 100$$
$$= 100.00\%$$

$$|\epsilon_a|_3 = \left| \frac{3.0923 - 1}{3.0923} \right| \times 100$$
$$= 67.662\%$$

The maximum absolute relative approximate error is 100.00%

Iteration #2

$$x_1 = \frac{1 - 3(4.9000) + 5(3.0923)}{12}$$

$$= 0.14679$$

$$x_2 = \frac{28 - (0.14679) - 3(3.0923)}{5}$$

$$= 3.7153$$

$$x_3 = \frac{76 - 3(0.14679) - 7(3.7153)}{13}$$

$$= 3.8118$$

At the end of second iteration, the absolute relative approximate error is

$$\left|\in_a\right|_1 = \left|\frac{0.14679 - 0.50000}{0.14679}\right| \times 100$$

$$= 240.61\%$$

$$\left|\in_a\right|_2 = \left|\frac{3.7153 - 4.9000}{3.7153}\right| \times 100$$

$$= 31.889\%$$

$$\left|\in_a\right|_3 = \left|\frac{3.8118 - 3.0923}{3.8118}\right| \times 100$$

$$= 18.874\%$$

The maximum absolute relative approximate error is 240.61%. This is greater than the value of 100.00% we obtained in the first iteration. Is the solution diverging? No, as you conduct more iterations, the solution converges as follows.

Iteration	x_1	$\left|\in_a\right|_1\%$	x_2	$\left|\in_a\right|_2\%$	x_3	$\left|\in_a\right|_3\%$
1	0.50000	100.00	4.9000	100.00	3.0923	67.662
2	0.14679	240.61	3.7153	31.889	3.8118	18.874
3	0.74275	80.236	3.1644	17.408	3.9708	4.0064
4	0.94675	21.546	3.0281	4.4996	3.9971	0.65772
5	0.99177	4.5391	3.0034	0.82499	4.0001	0.074383
6	0.99919	0.74307	3.0001	0.10856	4.0001	0.00101

This is close to the exact solution vector of

$$\begin{bmatrix} x_1 \\ x_2 \\ x_3 \end{bmatrix} = \begin{bmatrix} 1 \\ 3 \\ 4 \end{bmatrix}$$

Example 3

Given the system of equations

$$3x_1 + 7x_2 + 13x_3 = 76$$

$$x_1 + 5x_2 + 3x_3 = 28$$
$$12x_1 + 3x_2 - 5x_3 = 1$$

find the solution using the Gauss-Seidel method. Use

$$\begin{bmatrix} x_1 \\ x_2 \\ x_3 \end{bmatrix} = \begin{bmatrix} 1 \\ 0 \\ 1 \end{bmatrix}$$

as the initial guess.

Solution

Rewriting the equations, we get

$$x_1 = \frac{76 - 7x_2 - 13x_3}{3}$$

$$x_2 = \frac{28 - x_1 - 3x_3}{5}$$

$$x_3 = \frac{1 - 12x_1 - 3x_2}{-5}$$

Assuming an initial guess of

$$\begin{bmatrix} x_1 \\ x_2 \\ x_3 \end{bmatrix} = \begin{bmatrix} 1 \\ 0 \\ 1 \end{bmatrix}$$

the next six iterative values are given in the table below.

Iteration	x_1	$\left|\in_a\right|_1\%$	x_2	$\left|\in_a\right|_2\%$	x_3	$\left|\in_a\right|_3\%$
1	21.000	95.238	0.80000	100.00	50.680	98.027
2	−196.15	110.71	14.421	94.453	−462.30	110.96
3	1995.0	109.83	−116.02	112.43	4718.1	109.80
4	−20149	109.90	1204.6	109.63	−47636	109.90
5	2.0364×10^5	109.89	−12140	109.92	4.8144×10^5	109.89
6	-2.0579×10^6	109.89	1.2272×10^5	109.89	-4.8653×10^6	109.89

You can see that this solution is not converging and the coefficient matrix is not diagonally dominant. The coefficient matrix

$$[A] = \begin{bmatrix} 3 & 7 & 13 \\ 1 & 5 & 3 \\ 12 & 3 & -5 \end{bmatrix}$$

is not diagonally dominant as

$$|a_{11}| = |3| = 3 \le |a_{12}| + |a_{13}| = |7| + |13| = 20$$

Hence, the Gauss-Seidel method may or may not converge.

However, it is the same set of equations as the previous example and that converged. The only difference is that we exchanged first and the third equation with each other and that made the coefficient matrix not diagonally dominant.

Therefore, it is possible that a system of equations can be made diagonally dominant if one exchanges the equations with each other. However, it is not possible for all cases. For example, the following set of equations

$$x_1 + x_2 + x_3 = 3$$
$$2x_1 + 3x_2 + 4x_3 = 9$$
$$x_1 + 7x_2 + x_3 = 9$$

cannot be rewritten to make the coefficient matrix diagonally dominant.

Key Terms:

Gauss-Seidel method
Convergence of Gauss-Seidel method
Diagonally dominant matrix

Problem Set

Chapter 04.08
Gauss Siedel Method

1. In a system of equation [A] [X] = [C], if [A] is diagonally dominant, then Gauss-Seidel method
   (A) always converges
   (B) may or may not converge
   (C) always diverges

2. In a system of equations [A] [X] = [C], if [A] is not diagonally dominant, then Gauss-Seidel method
   (A) Always converges
   (B) May or may not converge
   (C) Always diverges.

3. In a system of equations [A] [X] = [C], if [A] is not diagonally dominant, the system of equations can always be rewritten to make it diagonally dominant.
   (A) True
   (B) False

4. Solve the following system of equations   using Gauss-Seidel method
$$12x_1 + 7x_2 + 3x_3 = 2$$
$$x_1 + 5x_2 + x_3 = -5$$
$$2x_1 + 7x_2 - 11x_3 = 6$$

   Conduct 3 iterations, calculate the maximum absolute relative approximate error at the end of each iteration and choose $\begin{bmatrix} x_1 & x_2 & x_3 \end{bmatrix} = \begin{bmatrix} 1 & 3 & 5 \end{bmatrix}$ as your initial guess.

5. Solve the following system of equations using Gauss-Seidel method
$$12x_1 + 7x_2 + 3x_3 = 2$$
$$x_1 + 5x_2 + x_3 = -5$$
$$2x_1 + 7x_2 - 11x_3 = 6$$

   Conduct 3 iterations, calculate the maximum absolute relative approximate error at the end of each iteration, and choose $\begin{bmatrix} x_1 & x_2 & x_3 \end{bmatrix} = \begin{bmatrix} 1 & 3 & 5 \end{bmatrix}$ as your initial guess.

6. Solve the following system of equations using Gauss-Seidel Method
$$x_1 + 5x_2 + x_3 = 5$$
$$12x_1 + 7x_2 + 3x_3 = 2$$
$$2x_1 + 7x_2 - 11x_3 = 6$$

04.08.1

Conduct 3 iterations, calculate the maximum absolute relative approximate error at the end of each iteration, and choose $[x_1 \quad x_2 \quad x_3] = [1 \quad 3 \quad 5]$ as your initial guess.

Answers to Selected Problems:

1. A

2. B

3. B

4. $\begin{bmatrix} x_1 & x_2 & x_3 \end{bmatrix} = \begin{bmatrix} 0.90666 & -1.0115 & -1.0243 \end{bmatrix}$

   $\begin{bmatrix} |\in_a|_1 & |\in_a|_2 & |\in_a|_3 \end{bmatrix} = \begin{bmatrix} 65.001\% & 10.564\% & 17.099\% \end{bmatrix}$

   $\begin{bmatrix} |\in_a|_1 & |\in_a|_2 & |\in_a|_3 \end{bmatrix} = \begin{bmatrix} 65.001\% & 10.564\% & 17.099\% \end{bmatrix}$

5. $\begin{bmatrix} x_1 & x_2 & x_3 \end{bmatrix} = \begin{bmatrix} 0.90666 & -1.0115 & -1.0243 \end{bmatrix}$

6. $\begin{bmatrix} x_1 & x_2 & x_3 \end{bmatrix} = \begin{bmatrix} -1163.7 & 1947.6 & 1027.2 \end{bmatrix}$

   $\begin{bmatrix} |\in_a|_1 & |\in_a|_2 & |\in_a|_3 \end{bmatrix} = \begin{bmatrix} 89.156\% & 89.139\% & 89.183\% \end{bmatrix}$

Chapter 04.09
Adequacy of Solutions

After reading this chapter, you should be able to:
1. *know the difference between ill-conditioned and well-conditioned systems of equations,*
2. *define the norm of a matrix, and*
3. *relate the norm of a matrix and of its inverse to the ill or well conditioning of the matrix, that is, how much trust can you having in the solution of the matrix.*

What do you mean by ill-conditioned and well-conditioned system of equations?

A system of equations is considered to be **well-conditioned** if a small change in the coefficient matrix or a small change in the right hand side results in a small change in the solution vector.

A system of equations is considered to be **ill-conditioned** if a small change in the coefficient matrix or a small change in the right hand side results in a large change in the solution vector.

Example 1

Is this system of equations well-conditioned?

$$\begin{bmatrix} 1 & 2 \\ 2 & 3.999 \end{bmatrix}\begin{bmatrix} x \\ y \end{bmatrix} = \begin{bmatrix} 4 \\ 7.999 \end{bmatrix}$$

Solution

The solution to the above set of equations is

$$\begin{bmatrix} x \\ y \end{bmatrix} = \begin{bmatrix} 2 \\ 1 \end{bmatrix}$$

Make a small change in the right hand side vector of the equations

04.09.1

$$\begin{bmatrix} 1 & 2 \\ 2 & 3.999 \end{bmatrix}\begin{bmatrix} x \\ y \end{bmatrix} = \begin{bmatrix} 4.001 \\ 7.998 \end{bmatrix}$$

gives

$$\begin{bmatrix} x \\ y \end{bmatrix} = \begin{bmatrix} -3.999 \\ 4.000 \end{bmatrix}$$

Make a small change in the coefficient matrix of the equations

$$\begin{bmatrix} 1.001 & 2.001 \\ 2.001 & 3.998 \end{bmatrix}\begin{bmatrix} x \\ y \end{bmatrix} = \begin{bmatrix} 4 \\ 7.999 \end{bmatrix}$$

gives

$$\begin{bmatrix} x \\ y \end{bmatrix} = \begin{bmatrix} 3.994 \\ 0.001388 \end{bmatrix}$$

This last systems of equation "looks" ill-conditioned because a small change in the coefficient matrix or the right hand side resulted in a large change in the solution vector.

Example 2

Is this system of equations well-conditioned?

$$\begin{bmatrix} 1 & 2 \\ 2 & 3 \end{bmatrix}\begin{bmatrix} x \\ y \end{bmatrix} = \begin{bmatrix} 4 \\ 7 \end{bmatrix}$$

Solution

The solution to the above equations is

$$\begin{bmatrix} x \\ y \end{bmatrix} = \begin{bmatrix} 2 \\ 1 \end{bmatrix}$$

Make a small change in the right hand side vector of the equations.

$$\begin{bmatrix} 1 & 2 \\ 2 & 3 \end{bmatrix}\begin{bmatrix} x \\ y \end{bmatrix} = \begin{bmatrix} 4.001 \\ 7.001 \end{bmatrix}$$

gives

$$\begin{bmatrix} x \\ y \end{bmatrix} = \begin{bmatrix} 1.999 \\ 1.001 \end{bmatrix}$$

Make a small change in the coefficient matrix of the equations.

$$\begin{bmatrix} 1.001 & 2.001 \\ 2.001 & 3.001 \end{bmatrix}\begin{bmatrix} x \\ y \end{bmatrix} = \begin{bmatrix} 4 \\ 7 \end{bmatrix}$$

gives

$$\begin{bmatrix} x \\ y \end{bmatrix} = \begin{bmatrix} 2.003 \\ 0.997 \end{bmatrix}$$

This system of equation "looks" well conditioned because small changes in the coefficient matrix or the right hand side resulted in small changes in the solution vector.

So what if the system of equations is ill conditioned or well conditioned?

Well, if a system of equations is ill-conditioned, we cannot trust the solution as much. Revisit the velocity problem, Example 5.1 in Chapter 5. The values in the coefficient matrix $[A]$ are squares of time, etc. For example, if instead of $a_{11} = 25$, you used $a_{11} = 24.99$, would you want this small change to make a huge difference in the solution vector. If it did, would you trust the solution?

Later we will see how much (quantifiable terms) we can trust the solution in a system of equations. Every invertible square matrix has a **condition number** and coupled with the **machine epsilon**, we can quantify how many significant digits one can trust in the solution.

To calculate the condition number of an invertible square matrix, I need to know what the norm of a matrix means. How is the norm of a matrix defined?

Just like the determinant, the norm of a matrix is a simple unique scalar number. However, the norm is always positive and is defined for all matrices – square or rectangular, and invertible or noninvertible square matrices.
One of the popular definitions of a norm is the row sum norm (also called the uniform-matrix norm). For a $m \times n$ matrix $[A]$, the row sum norm of $[A]$ is defined as

$$\|A\|_{\infty} = \max_{1 \le i \le m} \sum_{j=1}^{n} |a_{ij}|$$

that is, find the sum of the absolute value of the elements of each row of the matrix $[A]$. The maximum out of the m such values is the row sum norm of the matrix $[A]$.

Example 3

Find the row sum norm of the following matrix [A].

$$A = \begin{bmatrix} 10 & -7 & 0 \\ -3 & 2.099 & 6 \\ 5 & -1 & 5 \end{bmatrix}$$

Solution

$$\|A\|_\infty = \max_{1\le i\le 3} \sum_{j=1}^{3} |a_{ij}|$$
$$= \max\left[\left(|10|+|-7|+|0|\right),\left(|-3|+|2.099|+|6|\right),\left(|5|+|-1|+|5|\right)\right]$$
$$= \max\left[(10+7+0),(3+2.099+6),(5+1+5)\right]$$
$$= \max\left[17,11.099,11\right]$$
$$= 17.$$

How is the norm related to the conditioning of the matrix?

Let us start answering this question using an example. Go back to the *ill-conditioned* system of equations,

$$\begin{bmatrix} 1 & 2 \\ 2 & 3.999 \end{bmatrix}\begin{bmatrix} x \\ y \end{bmatrix} = \begin{bmatrix} 4 \\ 7.999 \end{bmatrix}$$

that gives the solution as

$$\begin{bmatrix} x \\ y \end{bmatrix} = \begin{bmatrix} 2 \\ 1 \end{bmatrix}$$

Denoting the above set of equations as

$$[A][X]=[C]$$
$$\|X\|_\infty = 2$$
$$\|C\|_\infty = 7.999$$

Making a small change in the right hand side,

$$\begin{bmatrix} 1 & 2 \\ 2 & 3.999 \end{bmatrix}\begin{bmatrix} x \\ y \end{bmatrix} = \begin{bmatrix} 4.001 \\ 7.998 \end{bmatrix}$$

gives

$$\begin{bmatrix} x \\ y \end{bmatrix} = \begin{bmatrix} -3.999 \\ 4.000 \end{bmatrix}$$

Denoting the above set of equations by

$$[A][X']=[C']$$

right hand side vector is found by

$$[\Delta C]=[C']-[C]$$

and the change in the solution vector is found by

$$[\Delta X]=[X']-[X]$$

then

$$[\Delta C] = \begin{bmatrix} 4.001 \\ 7.998 \end{bmatrix} - \begin{bmatrix} 4 \\ 7.999 \end{bmatrix}$$

$$= \begin{bmatrix} 0.001 \\ -0.001 \end{bmatrix}$$

and

$$[\Delta X] = \begin{bmatrix} -3.999 \\ 4.000 \end{bmatrix} - \begin{bmatrix} 2 \\ 1 \end{bmatrix}$$

$$= \begin{bmatrix} -5.999 \\ 3.000 \end{bmatrix}$$

then

$$\|\Delta C\|_\infty = 0.001$$

$$\|\Delta X\|_\infty = 5.999$$

The relative change in the norm of the solution vector is

$$\frac{\|\Delta X\|_\infty}{\|X\|_\infty} = \frac{5.999}{2}$$

$$= 2.9995$$

The relative change in the norm of the right hand side vector is

$$\frac{\|\Delta C\|_\infty}{\|C\|_\infty} = \frac{0.001}{7.999}$$

$$= 1.250 \times 10^{-4}$$

See the small relative change of 1.250×10^{-4} in the right hand side vector results in a large relative change in the solution vector as 2.9995.

In fact, the ratio between the relative change in the norm of the solution vector and the relative change in the norm of the right hand side vector is

$$\frac{\|\Delta X\|_\infty / \|X\|_\infty}{\|\Delta C\|_\infty / \|C\|_\infty} = \frac{2.9995}{1.250 \times 10^{-4}}$$

$$= 23993$$

Let us now go back to the *well-conditioned* system of equations.

$$\begin{bmatrix} 1 & 2 \\ 2 & 3 \end{bmatrix} \begin{bmatrix} x \\ y \end{bmatrix} = \begin{bmatrix} 4 \\ 7 \end{bmatrix}$$

gives

$$\begin{bmatrix} x \\ y \end{bmatrix} = \begin{bmatrix} 2 \\ 1 \end{bmatrix}$$

Denoting the system of equations by

$$[A][X] = [C]$$

$$\|X\|_\infty = 2$$

$$\|C\|_\infty = 7$$

Making a small change in the right hand side vector

$$\begin{bmatrix} 1 & 2 \\ 2 & 3 \end{bmatrix} \begin{bmatrix} x \\ y \end{bmatrix} = \begin{bmatrix} 4.001 \\ 7.001 \end{bmatrix}$$

gives

$$\begin{bmatrix} x \\ y \end{bmatrix} = \begin{bmatrix} 1.999 \\ 1.001 \end{bmatrix}$$

Denoting the above set of equations by

$$[A][X'] = [C']$$

the change in the right hand side vector is then found by

$$[\Delta C] = [C'] - [C]$$

and the change in the solution vector is

$$[\Delta X] = [X'] - [X]$$

then

$$[\Delta C] = \begin{bmatrix} 4.001 \\ 7.001 \end{bmatrix} - \begin{bmatrix} 4 \\ 7 \end{bmatrix}$$

$$= \begin{bmatrix} 0.001 \\ 0.001 \end{bmatrix}$$

and

$$[\Delta X] = \begin{bmatrix} 1.999 \\ 1.001 \end{bmatrix} - \begin{bmatrix} 2 \\ 1 \end{bmatrix}$$

$$= \begin{bmatrix} -0.001 \\ 0.001 \end{bmatrix}$$

then

$$\|\Delta C\|_\infty = 0.001$$

$$\|\Delta X\|_\infty = 0.001$$

The relative change in the norm of solution vector is

$$\frac{\|\Delta X\|_\infty}{\|X\|_\infty} = \frac{0.001}{2}$$

$$= 5 \times 10^{-4}$$

The relative change in the norm of the right hand side vector is

$$\frac{\|\Delta C\|_\infty}{\|C\|_\infty} = \frac{0.001}{7}$$

$$= 1.429 \times 10^{-4}$$

See the small relative change the right hand side vector of 1.429×10^{-4} results in the small relative change in the solution vector of 5×10^{-4}.

In fact, the ratio between the relative change in the norm of the solution vector and the relative change in the norm of the right hand side vector is

$$\frac{\|\Delta X\|_\infty / \|X\|_\infty}{\|\Delta C\|_\infty / \|C\|_\infty} = \frac{5 \times 10^{-4}}{1.429 \times 10^{-4}}$$

$$= 3.5$$

What are some of the properties of norms?

1. For a matrix $[A]$, $\|A\| \geq 0$
2. For a matrix $[A]$ and a scalar k, $\|kA\| = |k| \|A\|$
3. For two matrices $[A]$ and $[B]$ of same order, $\|A + B\| \leq \|A\| + \|B\|$
4. For two matrices $[A]$ and $[B]$ that can be multiplied as $[A][B]$, $\|AB\| \leq \|A\| \|B\|$

Is there a general relationship that exists between $\|\Delta X\| / \|X\|$ and $\|\Delta C\| / \|C\|$ or between $\|\Delta X\| / \|X\|$ and $\|\Delta A\| / \|A\|$? If so, it could help us identify well-conditioned and ill conditioned system of equations.

If there is such a relationship, will it help us quantify the conditioning of the matrix? That is, will it tell us how many significant digits we could trust in the solution of a system of simultaneous linear equations?

There is a relationship that exists between

$$\frac{\|\Delta X\|}{\|X\|} \text{ and } \frac{\|\Delta C\|}{\|C\|}$$

and between

$$\frac{\|\Delta X\|}{\|X\|} \text{ and } \frac{\|\Delta A\|}{\|A\|}$$

These relationships are

$$\frac{\|\Delta X\|}{\|X + \Delta X\|} \le \|A\|\|A^{-1}\|\frac{\|\Delta C\|}{\|C\|}$$

and

$$\frac{\|\Delta X\|}{\|X\|} \le \|A\|\|A^{-1}\|\frac{\|\Delta A\|}{\|A\|}$$

The above two inequalities show that the relative change in the norm of the right hand side vector or the coefficient matrix can be amplified by as much as $\|A\|\|A^{-1}\|$.

This number $\|A\|\|A^{-1}\|$ is called the **condition number** of the matrix and coupled with the machine epsilon, we can quantify the accuracy of the solution of $[A][X] = [C]$.

Prove for

$$[A][X] = [C]$$

that

$$\frac{\|\Delta X\|}{\|X + \Delta X\|} \le \|A\|\|A^{-1}\|\frac{\|\Delta A\|}{\|A\|}.$$

Proof

Let

$$[A][X] = [C] \tag{1}$$

Then if $[A]$ is changed to $[A']$, the $[X]$ will change to $[X']$, such that

$$[A'][X'] = [C] \tag{2}$$

From Equations (1) and (2),

$$[A][X] = [A'][X']$$

Denoting change in $[A]$ and $[X]$ matrices as $[\Delta A]$ and $[\Delta X]$, respectively

$$[\Delta A] = [A'] - [A]$$
$$[\Delta X] = [X'] - [X]$$

then
$$[A][X] = ([A]+[\Delta A])([X]+[\Delta X])$$
Expanding the above expression
$$[A][X] = [A][X]+[A][\Delta X]+[\Delta A][X]+[\Delta A][\Delta X]$$
$$[0] = [A][\Delta X]+[\Delta A]([X]+[\Delta X])$$
$$-[A][\Delta X] = [\Delta A]([X]+[\Delta X])$$
$$[\Delta X] = -[A]^{-1}[\Delta A]([X]+[\Delta X])$$
Applying the theorem of norms, that the norm of multiplied matrices is less than the multiplication of the individual norms of the matrices,
$$\|\Delta X\| \le \|A^{-1}\|\|\Delta A\|\|X+\Delta X\|$$
Multiplying both sides by $\|A\|$
$$\|A\|\|\Delta X\| \le \|A\|\|A^{-1}\|\|\Delta A\|\|X+\Delta X\|$$
$$\frac{\|\Delta X\|}{\|X+\Delta X\|} \le \|A\|\|A^{-1}\|\frac{\|\Delta A\|}{\|A\|}$$

How do I use the above theorems to find how many significant digits are correct in my solution vector?

The relative error in a solution vector is $\le$ Cond (A) $\times$ relative error in right hand side. The possible relative error in the solution vector is $\le$ Cond (A) $\times \in_{mach}$

Hence Cond (A) $\times \in_{mach}$ should give us the number of significant digits, m at least correct in our solution by comparing it with 0.5×10^{-m}.

Example 4

How many significant digits can I trust in the solution of the following system of equations?
$$\begin{bmatrix} 1 & 2 \\ 2 & 3.999 \end{bmatrix}\begin{bmatrix} x \\ y \end{bmatrix} = \begin{bmatrix} 2 \\ 4 \end{bmatrix}$$

Solution

For
$$[A] = \begin{bmatrix} 1 & 2 \\ 2 & 3.999 \end{bmatrix}$$
it can be shown

$$[A]^{-1} = \begin{bmatrix} -3999 & 2000 \\ 2000 & -1000 \end{bmatrix}$$

$$\|A\|_\infty = 5.999$$

$$\left\|A^{-1}\right\|_\infty = 5999$$

$$Cond(A) = \|A\|_\infty \left\|A^{-1}\right\|_\infty$$

$$= 5.999 \times 5999.4$$

$$= 35990$$

Assuming single precision with 24 bits used in the mantissa for real numbers, the machine epsilon is

$$\in_{mach} = 2^{1-24}$$

$$= 0.119209 \times 10^{-6}$$

$$Cond(A) \times \in_{mach} = 35990 \times 0.119209 \times 10^{-6}$$

$$= 0.4290 \times 10^{-2}$$

Comparing it with 0.5×10^{-m}

$$0.5 \times 10^{-m} < 0.4290 \times 10^{-2}$$

$m \leq 2$

So two significant digits are at least correct in the solution vector.

Example 5

How many significant digits can I trust in the solution of the following system of equations?

$$\begin{bmatrix} 1 & 2 \\ 2 & 3 \end{bmatrix} \begin{bmatrix} x \\ y \end{bmatrix} = \begin{bmatrix} 4 \\ 7 \end{bmatrix}$$

Solution

For

$$[A] = \begin{bmatrix} 1 & 2 \\ 2 & 3 \end{bmatrix}$$

it can be shown

$$[A]^{-1} = \begin{bmatrix} -3 & 2 \\ 2 & -1 \end{bmatrix}$$

Then

$$\|A\|_\infty = 5,$$

$$\|A^{-1}\|_{\infty} = 5.$$

$$\text{Cond}(A) = \|A\|_{\infty}\|A^{-1}\|_{\infty}$$
$$= 5 \times 5$$
$$= 25$$

Assuming single precision with 24 bits used in the mantissa for real numbers, the machine epsilon

$$\epsilon_{mach} = 2^{1-24}$$
$$= 0.119209 \times 10^{-6}$$
$$\text{Cond}(A) \times \epsilon_{mach} = 25 \times 0.119209 \times 10^{-6}$$
$$= 0.2980 \times 10^{-5}$$

Comparing it with 0.5×10^{-m}

$$0.5 \times 10^{-m} \leq 0.2980 \times 10^{-5}$$

$$m \leq 5$$

So five significant digits are at least correct in the solution vector.

Key Terms:

Ill-Conditioned matrix
Well-Conditioned matrix
Norm
Condition Number
Machine Epsilon
Significant Digits

Problem Set

Chapter 04.09
Adequacy of Solutions

1. The adequacy of the solution of simultaneous linear equations depends on
   (A) Condition number
   (B) Machine epsilon
   (C) Product of condition number and machine epsilon
   (D) Norm of the matrix.

2. If a system of equations $[A][X] = [C]$ is ill conditioned, then
   (A) $\det(A) = 0$
   (B) $\text{Cond}(A) = 1$
   (C) $\text{Cond}(A)$ is large.
   (D) $\|A\|$ is large.

3. If $\text{Cond}(A) = 10^4$ and $\in_{mach} = 0.119 \times 10^{-6}$, then in $[A][X] = [C]$, at least these many significant digits are correct in your solution,
   (A) 0
   (B) 1
   (C) 2
   (D) 3

Make a small change in the coefficient matrix of $\begin{bmatrix} 1 & 2 \\ 2 & 3.999 \end{bmatrix} \begin{bmatrix} x \\ y \end{bmatrix} = \begin{bmatrix} 4 \\ 7.999 \end{bmatrix}$

find

$$\frac{\|\Delta X\|_{\infty} / \|X\|_{\infty}}{4\|_{\infty} / \|A\|_{\infty}}$$

small number? How is this number related to the condition number matrix?

5. Make a small change in the coefficient matrix of

$$\begin{bmatrix} 1 & 2 \\ 2 & 3 \end{bmatrix} \begin{bmatrix} x \\ y \end{bmatrix} = \begin{bmatrix} 4 \\ 7 \end{bmatrix}$$

and find

$$\frac{\|\Delta X\|_\infty / \|X\|_\infty}{\|\Delta A\|_\infty / \|A\|_\infty}.$$

Is it a large or a small number? Compare your results with the previous problem. How is this number related to the condition number of the coefficient matrix?

6. Prove

$$\frac{\|\Delta X\|}{\|X\|} \le \|A\| \|A^{-1}\| \frac{\|\Delta C\|}{\|C\|}$$

7. For

$$[A] = \begin{bmatrix} 10 & -7 & 0 \\ -3 & 2.099 & 6 \\ 5 & -1 & 5 \end{bmatrix}$$

gives

$$[A]^{-1} = \begin{bmatrix} -0.1099 & -0.2333 & 0.2799 \\ -0.2999 & -0.3332 & 0.3999 \\ 0.04995 & 0.1666 & 6.664 \times 10^{-5} \end{bmatrix}$$

(A) What is the condition number of $[A]$?

(B) How many significant digits can we at least trust in the solution of $[A][X] = [C]$ if $\epsilon_{mach} = 0.1192 \times 10^{-6}$?

(C) Without calculating the inverse of the matrix $[A]$, can you estimate the condition number of $[A]$ using the theorem in problem#6?

8. Prove that the $Cond(A) \ge 1$.

Answers to Selected Problems:

1. C

2. C

3. C

4. Changing $[A]$ to
$$\begin{bmatrix} 1.001 & 2.001 \\ 2.001 & 4.000 \end{bmatrix}$$
Results in solution of
$$\begin{bmatrix} 5999 \\ -2999 \end{bmatrix}$$

$$\frac{\|\Delta X\|_\infty / \|X\|_\infty}{\|\Delta A\|_\infty / \|A\|_\infty} = \frac{5999.7 / 2}{0.002 / 5.999}$$

$$= 8.994 \times 10^6$$

5. Changing $[A]$ to
$$\begin{bmatrix} 1.001 & 2.001 \\ 2.001 & 3.000 \end{bmatrix}$$
Results in solution of
$$\begin{bmatrix} 2.003 \\ 0.9970 \end{bmatrix}$$

$$\frac{\|\Delta X\|_\infty / \|X\|_\infty}{\|\Delta A\|_\infty / \|A\|_\infty} = \frac{0.003 / 2.000}{0.002 / 5}$$

$$= 3.75$$

6. Use theorem that if $[A][B] = [C]$ then $\|A\|\|B\| \geq \|C\|$

7.
   (A) $\|A\| = 17$

        $\|A^{-1}\| = 1.033$

        Cond (A) = 17.56

   (B) 5

   (C) Try different values of right hand side of $C = [\pm 1 \ \pm 1 \ \pm 1]^{\mathrm{T}}$ with signs chosen randomly. Then $\|A^{-1}\| \leq \|X\|$ obtained from solving equation set $[A][X] = [C]$ as $\|C\| = 1$.

8. We know that

        $$\|A\,B\| \leq \|A\| \|B\|$$

    then if

        $$[B] = [A]^{-1},$$

        $$\|A\,A^{-1}\| \leq \|A\| \|A^{-1}\|$$

        $$\|I\| \leq \|A\| \|A^{-1}\|$$

        $$1 \leq \|A\| \|A^{-1}\|$$

        $$\|A\| \|A^{-1}\| \geq 1$$

        $$Cond(A) \geq 1$$

Chapter 04.10
Eigenvalues and Eigenvectors

After reading this chapter, you should be able to:

1. *define eigenvalues and eigenvectors of a square matrix,*
2. *find eigenvalues and eigenvectors of a square matrix,*
3. *relate eigenvalues to the singularity of a square matrix, and*
4. *use the power method to numerically find the largest eigenvalue in magnitude of a square matrix and the corresponding eigenvector.*

What does eigenvalue mean?

The word eigenvalue comes from the German word *Eigenwert* where Eigen means *characteristic* and Wert means *value*. However, what the word means is not on your mind! You want to know why I need to learn about eigenvalues and eigenvectors. Once I give you an example of an application of eigenvalues and eigenvectors, you will want to know how to find these eigenvalues and eigenvectors.

Can you give me a physical example application of eigenvalues and eigenvectors?

Look at the spring-mass system as shown in the picture below.

Assume each of the two mass-displacements to be denoted by x_1 and x_2, and let us assume each spring has the same spring constant k. Then by applying Newton's 2nd and 3rd law of motion to develop a force-balance for each mass we have

$$m_1 \frac{d^2 x_1}{dt^2} = -kx_1 + k(x_2 - x_1)$$

$$m_2 \frac{d^2 x_2}{dt^2} = -k(x_2 - x_1)$$

Rewriting the equations, we have

$$m_1 \frac{d^2 x_1}{dt^2} - k(-2x_1 + x_2) = 0$$

$$m_2 \frac{d^2 x_2}{dt^2} - k(x_1 - x_2) = 0$$

Let $m_1 = 10, m_2 = 20, k = 15$

$$10 \frac{d^2 x_1}{dt^2} - 15(-2x_1 + x_2) = 0$$

$$20 \frac{d^2 x_2}{dt^2} - 15(x_1 - x_2) = 0$$

From vibration theory, the solutions can be of the form

$$x_i = A_i \sin(\omega t - \emptyset)$$

where

A_i = amplitude of the vibration of mass i,

ω = frequency of vibration,

$\emptyset$ = phase shift.

then

$$\frac{d^2 x_i}{dt^2} = -A_i w^2 Sin(\omega t - \emptyset)$$

Substituting x_i and $\frac{d^2 x_i}{dt^2}$ in equations,

$$-10 A_1 \omega^2 - 15(-2A_1 + A_2) = 0$$

$$-20 A_2 \omega^2 - 15(A_1 - A_2) = 0$$

gives

$$(-10\omega^2 + 30)A_1 - 15 A_2 = 0$$

$$-15 A_1 + (-20\omega^2 + 15)A_2 = 0$$

or

$$(-\omega^2 + 3)A_1 - 1.5 A_2 = 0$$

$$-0.75 A_1 + (-\omega^2 + 0.75)A_2 = 0$$

In matrix form, these equations can be rewritten as

$$\begin{bmatrix} -\omega^2 + 3 & -1.5 \\ -0.75 & -\omega^2 + 0.75 \end{bmatrix} \begin{bmatrix} A_1 \\ A_2 \end{bmatrix} = \begin{bmatrix} 0 \\ 0 \end{bmatrix}$$

$$\begin{bmatrix} 3 & -1.5 \\ -0.75 & 0.75 \end{bmatrix} \begin{bmatrix} A_1 \\ A_2 \end{bmatrix} - \omega^2 \begin{bmatrix} A_1 \\ A_2 \end{bmatrix} = \begin{bmatrix} 0 \\ 0 \end{bmatrix}$$

Let $\omega^2 = \lambda$

$$[A] = \begin{bmatrix} 3 & -1.5 \\ -0.75 & 0.75 \end{bmatrix}$$

$$[X] = \begin{bmatrix} A_1 \\ A_2 \end{bmatrix}$$

$$[A][X] - \lambda[X] = 0$$

$$[A][X] = \lambda[X]$$

In the above equation, λ is the eigenvalue and $[X]$ is the eigenvector corresponding to λ. As you can see, if we know λ for the above example we can calculate the natural frequency of the vibration

$$\omega = \sqrt{\lambda}$$

Why are the natural frequencies of vibration important? Because you do not want to have a forcing force on the spring-mass system close to this frequency as it would make the amplitude A_i very large and make the system unstable.

What is the general definition of eigenvalues and eigenvectors of a square matrix?

If $[A]$ is a $n \times n$ matrix, then $[X] \neq \bar{0}$ is an eigenvector of $[A]$ if

$$[A][X] = \lambda[X]$$

where λ is a scalar and $[X] \neq 0$. The scalar λ is called the eigenvalue of $[A]$ and $[A]$ is called the eigenvector corresponding to the eigenvalue λ.

How do I find eigenvalues of a square matrix?

To find the eigenvalues of a $n \times n$ matrix $[A]$, we have

$$[A][X] = \lambda[X]$$

$$[A][X] - \lambda[X] = 0$$

$$[A][X] - \lambda[I][X] = 0$$

$$([A] - [\lambda][I])[X] = 0$$

Now for the above set of equations to have a nonzero solution,

$$\det([A] - \lambda[I]) = 0$$

This left hand side can be expanded to give a polynomial in λ solving the above equation would give us values of the eigenvalues. The above equation is called the characteristic equation of $[A]$.

For a $[A]$ $n \times n$ matrix, the characteristic polynomial of A is of degree n as follows

$$\det([A] - \lambda[I]) = 0$$

giving

$$\lambda^n + c_1\lambda^{n-1} + c_2\lambda^{n-2} + - - + c_n = 0$$

Hence. this polynomial has n roots.

Example 1

Find the eigenvalues of the <u>physical problem discussed in the beginning of this chapter</u>, that is, find the eigenvalues of the matrix

$$[A] = \begin{bmatrix} 3 & -1.5 \\ -0.75 & 0.75 \end{bmatrix}$$

Solution

$$[A] - \lambda[I] = \begin{bmatrix} 3-\lambda & -1.5 \\ -0.75 & 0.75-\lambda \end{bmatrix}$$

$$\det([A] - \lambda[I]) = (3-\lambda)(0.75-\lambda) - (-0.75)(-1.5) = 0$$

$$2.25 - 0.75\lambda - 3\lambda + \lambda^2 - 1.125 = 0$$

$$\lambda^2 - 3.75\lambda + 1.125 = 0$$

$$\lambda = \frac{-(-3.75) \pm \sqrt{(-3.75)^2 - 4(1)(1.125)}}{2(1)}$$

$$= \frac{3.75 \pm 3.092}{2}$$

$$= 3.421, 0.3288$$

So the eigenvalues are 3.421 and 0.3288.

Example 2

Find the eigenvectors of

$$A = \begin{bmatrix} 3 & -1.5 \\ -0.75 & 0.75 \end{bmatrix}$$

Solution

The eigenvalues have already been found in Example 1 as

$$\lambda_1 = 3.421, \lambda_2 = 0.3288$$

Let

$$[X] = \begin{bmatrix} x_1 \\ x_2 \end{bmatrix}$$

be the eigenvector corresponding to

$$\lambda_1 = 3.421$$

Hence

$$([A] - \lambda_1[I])[X] = 0$$

$$\left\{ \begin{bmatrix} 3 & -1.5 \\ -0.75 & 0.75 \end{bmatrix} - 3.421 \begin{bmatrix} 1 & 0 \\ 0 & 1 \end{bmatrix} \right\} \begin{bmatrix} x_1 \\ x_2 \end{bmatrix} = 0$$

$$\begin{bmatrix} -0.421 & -1.5 \\ -0.75 & -2.671 \end{bmatrix} \begin{bmatrix} x_1 \\ x_2 \end{bmatrix} = \begin{bmatrix} 0 \\ 0 \end{bmatrix}$$

If

$$x_1 = s$$

then

$$-0.421s - 1.5x_2 = 0$$

$$x_2 = -0.2808s$$

The eigenvector corresponding to $\lambda_1 = 3.421$ then is

$$[X] = \begin{bmatrix} s \\ -0.2808s \end{bmatrix}$$

$$= s \begin{bmatrix} 1 \\ -0.2808 \end{bmatrix}$$

The eigenvector corresponding to

$$\lambda_1 = 3.421$$

is

$$\begin{bmatrix} 1 \\ -0.2808 \end{bmatrix}$$

Similarly, the eigenvector corresponding to

$$\lambda_2 = 0.3288$$

is

$$\begin{bmatrix} 1 \\ 1.781 \end{bmatrix}$$

Example 3

Find the eigenvalues and eigenvectors of

$$[A] = \begin{bmatrix} 1.5 & 0 & 1 \\ -0.5 & 0.5 & -0.5 \\ -0.5 & 0 & 0 \end{bmatrix}$$

Solution

The characteristic equation is given by

$$\det([A] - \lambda[I]) = 0$$

$$\det \begin{bmatrix} 1.5 - \lambda & 0 & 1 \\ -0.5 & 0.5 - \lambda & -0.5 \\ -0.5 & 0 & -\lambda \end{bmatrix} = 0$$

$$(1.5 - \lambda)[(0.5 - \lambda)(-\lambda) - (-0.5)(0)] + (1)[(-0.5)(0) - (-0.5)(0.5 - \lambda)] = 0$$

$$-\lambda^3 + 2\lambda^2 - 1.25\lambda = 0$$

The roots of the above equation are

$$\lambda = 0.5, 0.5, 1.0$$

Note that there are eigenvalues that are repeated. Since there are only two distinct eigenvalues, there are only two eigenspaces. But, corresponding to $\lambda = 0.5$ there should be two eigenvectors that form a basis for the eigenspace.

To find the eigenspaces, let

$$[X] = \begin{bmatrix} x_1 \\ x_2 \\ x_3 \end{bmatrix}$$

Given

$$[(A - \lambda I)][X] = 0$$

then

$$\begin{bmatrix} 1.5-\lambda & 0 & 1 \\ -0.5 & 0.5-\lambda & -0.5 \\ -0.5 & 0 & -\lambda \end{bmatrix}\begin{bmatrix} x_1 \\ x_2 \\ x_3 \end{bmatrix} = \begin{bmatrix} 0 \\ 0 \\ 0 \end{bmatrix}$$

For $\lambda = 0.5$,

$$\begin{bmatrix} 1 & 0 & 1 \\ -0.5 & 0 & -0.5 \\ -0.5 & 0 & -0.5 \end{bmatrix}\begin{bmatrix} x_1 \\ x_2 \\ x_3 \end{bmatrix} = \begin{bmatrix} 0 \\ 0 \\ 0 \end{bmatrix}$$

Solving this system gives

$$x_1 = -a, x_2 = b\, x_3 = a$$

So

$$\begin{bmatrix} x_1 \\ x_2 \\ x_3 \end{bmatrix} = \begin{bmatrix} -a \\ b \\ a \end{bmatrix}$$

$$= \begin{bmatrix} a \\ 0 \\ -a \end{bmatrix} + \begin{bmatrix} 0 \\ b \\ 0 \end{bmatrix}$$

$$= a\begin{bmatrix} 1 \\ 0 \\ -1 \end{bmatrix} + b\begin{bmatrix} 0 \\ 1 \\ 0 \end{bmatrix}$$

So the vectors $\begin{bmatrix} -1 \\ 0 \\ 1 \end{bmatrix}$ and $\begin{bmatrix} 0 \\ 1 \\ 0 \end{bmatrix}$ form a basis for the eigenspace for the eigenvalue $\lambda = 0.5$.

For $\lambda = 1$,

$$\begin{bmatrix} 0.5 & 0 & 1 \\ -0.5 & -0.5 & -0.5 \\ -0.5 & 0 & -1 \end{bmatrix}\begin{bmatrix} x_1 \\ x_2 \\ x_3 \end{bmatrix} = \begin{bmatrix} 0 \\ 0 \\ 0 \end{bmatrix}$$

Solving this system gives

$$x_1 = a, x_2 = -0.5a, x_3 = -0.5a$$

The eigenvector corresponding to $\lambda = 1$ is

$$\begin{bmatrix} a \\ -0.5a \\ -0.5a \end{bmatrix} = a\begin{bmatrix} 1 \\ -0.5 \\ -0.5 \end{bmatrix}$$

Hence the vector $\begin{bmatrix} 1 \\ -0.5 \\ -0.5 \end{bmatrix}$ is a basis for the eigenspace for the eigenvalue of $\lambda = 1$.

What are some of the theorems of eigenvalues and eigenvectors?

Theorem 1: If $[A]$ is a $n \times n$ triangular matrix – upper triangular, lower triangular or diagonal, the eigenvalues of $[A]$ are the diagonal entries of $[A]$.

Theorem 2: $\lambda = 0$ is an eigenvalue of $[A]$ if $[A]$ is a singular (noninvertible) matrix.

Theorem 3: $[A]$ and $[A]^{\mathrm{T}}$ have the same eigenvalues.

Theorem 4: Eigenvalues of a symmetric matrix are real.

Theorem 5: Eigenvectors of a symmetric matrix are orthogonal, but only for distinct eigenvalues.

Theorem 6: $\left|\det(A)\right|$ is the product of the absolute values of the eigenvalues of $[A]$.

Example 4

What are the eigenvalues of

$$[A] = \begin{bmatrix} 6 & 0 & 0 & 0 \\ 7 & 3 & 0 & 0 \\ 9 & 5 & 7.5 & 0 \\ 2 & 6 & 0 & -7.2 \end{bmatrix}$$

Solution

Since the matrix $[A]$ is a lower triangular matrix, the eigenvalues of $[A]$ are the diagonal elements of $[A]$. The eigenvalues are

$$\lambda_1 = 6, \lambda_2 = 3, \lambda_3 = 7.5, \lambda_4 = -7.2$$

Example 5

One of the eigenvalues of

$$[A] = \begin{bmatrix} 5 & 6 & 2 \\ 3 & 5 & 9 \\ 2 & 1 & -7 \end{bmatrix}$$

is zero. Is $[A]$ invertible?

Solution

$\lambda = 0$ is an eigenvalue of $[A]$, that implies $[A]$ is singular and is not invertible.

Example 6

Given the eigenvalues of

$$[A] = \begin{bmatrix} 2 & -3.5 & 6 \\ 3.5 & 5 & 2 \\ 8 & 1 & 8.5 \end{bmatrix}$$

are

$$\lambda_1 = -1.547, \lambda_2 = 12.33, \lambda_3 = 4.711$$

What are the eigenvalues of $[B]$ if

$$[B] = \begin{bmatrix} 2 & 3.5 & 8 \\ -3.5 & 5 & 1 \\ 6 & 2 & 8.5 \end{bmatrix}$$

Solution

Since $[B] = [A]^T$, the eigenvalues of $[A]$ and $[B]$ are the same. Hence eigenvalues of $[B]$ also are

$$\lambda_1 = -1.547, \lambda_2 = 12.33, \lambda_3 = 4.711$$

Example 7

Given the eigenvalues of

$$[A] = \begin{bmatrix} 2 & -3.5 & 6 \\ 3.5 & 5 & 2 \\ 8 & 1 & 8.5 \end{bmatrix}$$

are

$$\lambda_1 = -1.547, \lambda_2 = 12.33, \lambda_3 = 4.711$$

Calculate the magnitude of the determinant of the matrix.
Solution

Since

$$\begin{aligned} |\det[A]| &= |\lambda_1||\lambda_2||\lambda_3| \\ &= |-1.547||12.33||4.711| \\ &= 89.88 \end{aligned}$$

How does one find eigenvalues and eigenvectors numerically?

One of the most common methods used for finding eigenvalues and eigenvectors is the power method. It is used to find the largest eigenvalue in an absolute sense. Note that if this largest eigenvalues is repeated, this method will not work. Also this eigenvalue needs to be distinct. The method is as follows:

1. Assume a guess $[X^{(0)}]$ for the eigenvector in
   $$[A][X] = \lambda[X]$$
   equation. One of the entries of $[X^{(0)}]$ needs to be unity.

2. Find
   $$[Y^{(1)}] = [A][X^{(0)}]$$

3. Scale $[Y^{(1)}]$ so that the chosen unity component remains unity.
   $$[Y^{(1)}] = \lambda^{(1)}[X^{(1)}]$$

4. Repeat steps (2) and (3) with
   $$[X] = [X^{(1)}] \text{ to get } [X^{(2)}].$$

5. Repeat the steps 2 and 3 until the value of the eigenvalue converges.

If E_s is the pre-specified percentage relative error tolerance to which you would like the answer to converge to, keep iterating until

$$\left| \frac{\lambda^{(i+1)} - \lambda^{(i)}}{\lambda^{(i+1)}} \right| \times 100 \le E_s$$

where the left hand side of the above inequality is the definition of absolute percentage relative approximate error, denoted generally by E_s. A pre-specified percentage relative tolerance of $0.5 \times 10^{2-m}$ implies at least m significant digits are current in your answer. When the system converges, the value of λ is the largest (in absolute value) eigenvalue of $[A]$.

Example 8

Using the power method, find the largest eigenvalue and the corresponding eigenvector of

$$[A] = \begin{bmatrix} 1.5 & 0 & 1 \\ -0.5 & 0.5 & -0.5 \\ -0.5 & 0 & 0 \end{bmatrix}$$

Solution

Assume

$$[X^{(0)}] = \begin{bmatrix} 1 \\ 1 \\ 1 \end{bmatrix}$$

$$[A][X^{(0)}] = \begin{bmatrix} 1.5 & 0 & 1 \\ -0.5 & 0.5 & -0.5 \\ -0.5 & 0 & 0 \end{bmatrix} \begin{bmatrix} 1 \\ 1 \\ 1 \end{bmatrix}$$

$$= \begin{bmatrix} 2.5 \\ -0.5 \\ -0.5 \end{bmatrix}$$

$$Y^{(1)} = 2.5 \begin{bmatrix} 1 \\ -0.2 \\ -0.2 \end{bmatrix}$$

$$\lambda^{(1)} = 2.5$$

We will choose the first element of $[X^{(0)}]$ to be unity.

$$[X^{(1)}] = \begin{bmatrix} 1 \\ -0.2 \\ -0.2 \end{bmatrix}$$

$$[A][X^{(1)}] = \begin{bmatrix} 1.5 & 0 & 1 \\ -0.5 & 0.5 & -0.5 \\ -0.5 & 0 & 0 \end{bmatrix} \begin{bmatrix} 1 \\ -0.2 \\ -0.2 \end{bmatrix}$$

$$= \begin{bmatrix} 1.3 \\ -0.5 \\ -0.5 \end{bmatrix}$$

$$[X^{(2)}] = 1.3 \begin{bmatrix} 1 \\ -0.3846 \\ -0.3846 \end{bmatrix}$$

$$\lambda^{(2)} = 1.3$$

$$[X^{(2)}] = \begin{bmatrix} 1 \\ -0.3846 \\ -0.3846 \end{bmatrix}$$

The absolute relative approximate error in the eigenvalues is

$$|\varepsilon_a| = \left| \frac{\lambda^{(2)} - \lambda^{(1)}}{\lambda^{(2)}} \right| \times 100$$

$$= \left| \frac{1.3 - 1.5}{1.5} \right| \times 100$$

$$= 92.307\%$$

Conducting further iterations, the values of $\lambda^{(i)}$ and the corresponding eigenvectors is given in the table below

i	$\lambda^{(i)}$	$[X^{(i)}]$	$|\varepsilon_a|$ (%)
1	2.5	$\begin{bmatrix} 1 \\ -0.2 \\ -0.2 \end{bmatrix}$	____
2	1.3	$\begin{bmatrix} 1 \\ -0.38462 \\ -0.38462 \end{bmatrix}$	92.307
3	1.1154	$\begin{bmatrix} 1 \\ -0.44827 \\ -0.44827 \end{bmatrix}$	16.552
4	1.0517	$\begin{bmatrix} 1 \\ -0.47541 \\ -0.47541 \end{bmatrix}$	6.0529

5	1.02459	$\begin{bmatrix} 1 \\ -0.48800 \\ -0.48800 \end{bmatrix}$	1.2441

The exact value of the eigenvalue is $\lambda = 1$
and the corresponding eigenvector is

$$[X] = \begin{bmatrix} 1 \\ -0.5 \\ -0.5 \end{bmatrix}$$

Key Terms:

Eigenvalue
Eigenvectors
Power method

Problem Set

Chapter 04.10
Eigenvalues and Eigenvectors

1. The eigenvalues λ of matrix $[A]$ are found by solving the equation(s)?
   (A) $[A][X] = [I]$
   (B) $[A][X] - \lambda[I] = 0$
   (C) $|A = 0|$
   (D) $|A - \lambda I| = 0$

2. Find the eigenvalues and eigenvectors of
   $$[A] = \begin{bmatrix} 10 & 9 \\ 2 & 3 \end{bmatrix}$$
   using the determinant method

3. Find the eigenvalues and eigenvectors of
   $$[A] = \begin{bmatrix} 4 & 0 & 1 \\ -2 & 0 & 1 \\ 2 & 0 & 1 \end{bmatrix}$$
   using the determinant method

4. Find the eigenvalues of these matrices by inspection
   (A) $\begin{bmatrix} 2 & 0 & 0 \\ 0 & -3 & 0 \\ 0 & 0 & 6 \end{bmatrix}$

   (B) $\begin{bmatrix} 3 & 5 & 7 \\ 0 & -2 & 1 \\ 0 & 0 & 0 \end{bmatrix}$

   (C) $\begin{bmatrix} 2 & 0 & 0 \\ 3 & 5 & 0 \\ 2 & 1 & 6 \end{bmatrix}$

5. Find the largest eigenvalue in magnitude and its corresponding vector by using the power method

$$[A] = \begin{bmatrix} 4 & 0 & 1 \\ -2 & 0 & 1 \\ 2 & 0 & 1 \end{bmatrix}$$

Start with an initial guess of the eigenvector as

$$\begin{bmatrix} 1 \\ -0.5 \\ 0.5 \end{bmatrix}$$

6. Prove if λ is an eigenvalue of $[A]$, then $\dfrac{1}{\lambda}$ is an eigenvalue of $[A]^{-1}$.

7. Prove that square matrices $[A]$ and $[A]^T$ have the same eigenvalues.

8. Show that $\left| \det(A) \right|$ is the product of the absolute values of the eigenvalues of $[A]$.

Answers to Selected Problems:

1. D

2. $(12,1)$, $\begin{bmatrix} 0.9762 \\ 0.2169 \end{bmatrix}$, $\begin{bmatrix} 0.8381 \\ -0.8381 \end{bmatrix}$

3. $(0,4,5615,0.43845)$, $\begin{bmatrix} 0 \\ 1 \\ 0 \end{bmatrix}$, $\begin{bmatrix} 0.87193 \\ -0.27496 \\ 0.48963 \end{bmatrix}$, $\begin{bmatrix} -0.27816 \\ 3.5284 \\ 0.99068 \end{bmatrix}$

4.
   (A) $2, -3, 6$
   (B) $3, -2, 0$
   (C) $2, 5, 6$

5. 4.5615, $\begin{bmatrix} 1 \\ -0.31534 \\ 0.56154 \end{bmatrix}$ after 4 iterations

INDEX

R

Rank of a matrix, 64
Row Vector, 2, 13, 36, 45

S

Scalar Product of Matrices, 37
Singular, 71, 109, 160
Skew-Symmetric Matrix, 46
Square Matrix, 3, 4, 6, 46, 48, 52, 71, 72, 78, 104, 112, 118, 140, 156
Submatrix, 3, 48, 64
Subtraction of Matrices, 33
Symmetric Matrix, 46, 146
System of Equations, 61-78, 125, 130, 138, 140

T

Transpose, 45
Tridiagonal Matrices, 6

U

Unique Solution, 29, 63, 64, 69, 70
Unit Vector, 17
Upper Triangular Matrix, 4, 111, 115

V

Vector, 2, 13-27, 45, 63, 72, 146
see also Unit Vector
see also Null Vector
see also Row Vector

W

Well-Conditioned, 138, 142, 144

Z

Zero Matrix, 5
Zero Vector, 16, 21, 23, 83

CPSIA information can be obtained at www.ICGtesting.com
Printed in the USA
242062LV00001BA/26/P